MW00568157

State Fair Stories

the Days and People of the
New York State Fair

by
Judith LaManna Rivette

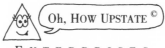

Oh, How Upstate ©

ENTERPRISES
Liverpool, New York
www.solvaystories.com

State Fair Stories: the Days and People of the New York State Fair.
Copyright © 2005 by Judith LaManna Rivette. Manufactured in the
United States of America. All rights reserved. No part of this book
may be reproduced in any form or by any means whatsoever – including electronic, mechanical, information storage and retrieval systems –
without permission in writing from the publisher, except that a review-
er may quote brief passages in a review. Published by Oh, How
Upstate© Enterprises, 200 Old Liverpool Road, Liverpool, NY 13088
(315) 478-1122 ext.17. First edition.
www.solvaystories.com

ISBN 978-0-9744046-2-2

LCCN 2005901801

First printing: August 2005

Writing, compilation, edit, cover design
by Judith LaManna Rivette

Layout and production by United Imaging and Printing,
Syracuse, NY

Dedication

To those who work together to make the Fair happen,
and make us happy.
To the diversity of people who come to the Fair
and are made happy.

Table of Contents

Preface, vii

Introduction, ix

From the Fair Director, x

A Brief History, 1

Signs of the Fair, 6

Admissions, 10

Competitions, 17

Exhibits, 26

Places, 33

Entertainment, 38

Races, 43

Food and Give-Aways, 47

Midway, 56

People, 62

Special Visitors, 71

Events, 74

Sports, 81

Work and Jobs, 85

Weather, 96

Fair Life, 101

The Experience, 106

The *State Fair Stories* Story, 118

Names Index, 121

Afterword, 129

About the Editor/Author, 131

Other Publications, 132

Preface

To New Yorkers, the story of the New York State Fair is a story about a mystical Village that emerges annually to our notice near the end of July, appears full of energy and excitement in late August and, after Labor Day, is gone.

The New York State Fair Grounds is a place, a geography. But the Fair is also a community with a history and life of its own. If its pulse is the annual event that now begins in late August, its blood stream is the people who maintain that pulse at the fairgrounds throughout the year. If its focus seems to most to be the Fair, its life is in all of its uses. It has its own rhythm. Visitors to its events – all events, and all people, in all shades of skin color, ages and interests – have their own routines and comforts. It is a place as well as an experience. It has neighborhoods, traditions. It has enthusiasms of all sorts, for all kinds of activities and at all different levels. It has memories.

As with my past books, the memories collected here are from "story-tellers" whose names appear at the end of their stories. In my editing, I tried to keep the style of each story-teller, but edit I had to do, along with re-writing or – in the case of oral submissions – writing. There are many photos in this book, with contributor names noted.

Credits appear with the photos. Abbreviations are used to credit repeated sources of material: photos by Jenna LaManna (JPL) and me (JLR), the collections of Fair memorabilia from Peter Cappuccilli (PC) and Nick Pirro, Jr. (NP) and the photos and materials from the Fair (SF), published with their permission – the work mostly by talented Fair Photographer Mike Okoniewski.

The story of this volume is in "The Story of State Fair Stories" chapter. The support for this effort from New York State Fair Director Peter Cappuccilli and his assistant, Joan Balduzzi Kerr, as well as from many of its employees and members of the public has been exceptional. I welcome back some of my previous story-tellers, with delight. The enthusiasm of Fair-goers has been exhilarating. But necessary, always, has been the proof-reading, cajoling support and assistance of my husband, Ric Rivette.

It's time, now, for our memories.

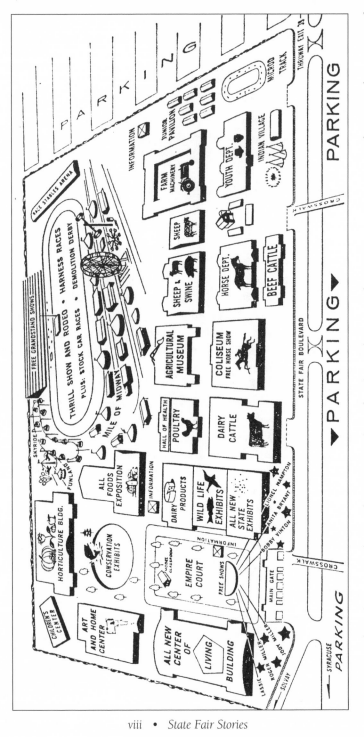

Tom Demperio drew this map to advertise the 1965 Fair, then referred to as the New York State "Exposition." It ran in the Metropolitan Section of the Herald-American with the caption "Here is the official guide map for the 1965 Exposition. Cut it out, save it, and take it along when you go."

Introduction

When we think about the New York State Fair Grounds, we think of the Fair, an event that takes place at the end of the summer involving rides, food, efforts at free entry, live performances of named stars and entertainers at the Grandstand and other places, food, parking and walking, food, walking, exhibits, people watching, competitions, fireworks and more food. Not to be forgotten in this seemingly endless list of activities are the butter sculpture, the NYS Drinking Water Taste Contest, a daily evening parade, beef and dairy cattle, goats and sheep, swine, llamas, rabbits, horse shows, living statues and cartoon character street entertainers, and many, many other items, locations and activities that you will stroll through in these pages. Did I mention the food?

Some of us have also come to think of the fairgrounds in recent years as a place for other events, tending toward our own special interests. There are Dog Shows, Cat Shows, Car Shows of all variety and ilk, Horse Shows and competitions independent of the Fair, Boat Shows, conventions of the Fire Department and other large groups. Large and regularly held craft shows, theater year round, Empire Room receptions both private and public and microd racing.

Many of us probably have little knowledge of the history of the Fair. Because I can't help myself, I want to share some of that history with you. In addition to the chapter that gives a brief history of the Fair, you will find historical references scattered in the various chapters. But you will also get a sense of that history, I think, in the pages full of memories that touch upon times past and events not contained in the late months of the summer.

I hope you enjoy this visit to the New York State Fair Grounds.

From the Fair Director

It is an unbelievable privilege to have been appointed by Governor George Pataki and to serve in his administration and to serve the residents of New York State as the Director of the Great New York State Fair. Additionally, it is an unbelievable privilege to work with so many dedicated, committed, wonderful people who help in so many ways to plan, prepare and present the Great New York State Fair as well as the hundreds of off-season events held at the fairgrounds year-round.

To all of you I say thank you from the bottom of my heart.

Also, I would like to thank Judith La Manna Rivette for her time in creating and developing

From the 1999 Fair, New York State Fair Director Peter Cappuccilli on the Midway. SF

this fun and historical book based on the memories of the many visitors and employees of the Fair.

I myself have many, many stories to share, not only from my past ten years as Director, but also as a kid working the Fair and as a Fairgoer. I will, however, save a couple of those stories for Judith's next volume and tell you in this volume the worst and best stories, which happen to be one in the same.

The worst story came at 1:20 a.m. on Labor Day, September 1998, when a wind shear tornado-like storm raced through the fairgrounds taking two lives, caused millions of dollars in damage and cancelled the last day of the State Fair.

The best story came in the following hours and days when our staff, Solvay Fire and Rescue, the New York State Police, the Red Cross, Rural Metro, the Governor, the Department of Agriculture and Markets, the local media and so many others worked together to flawlessly execute our emergency response plan, assist in the clean up of the catastrophe and help put the Fair back on its feet. Watching many in our community come together and roll up their sleeves to help in time of need is what makes us all proud to live and work in Syracuse and in our great State of New York.

That best story can only be rivaled by the thousands of smiles we see each year at the Fair, on the faces of our guests, especially persons with special needs and the underprivileged youth. I am truly blessed to be in a position to work together with so many talented people and to share in the opportunity to bring happiness to so many others. It is so rewarding.

Peter Cappuccilli, Jr.
Director
New York State Fair

A Brief History

Although we find ourselves treading into Dairy, Poultry, Horticulture and Agriculture Buildings with keen interest in the displays, we probably have lost track of the fact that this Fair – as with most fairs throughout time – began as a place where the farm and agriculture community displayed its wares, and showed off exceptional cattle, sheep, poultry and produce. It was where the latest in technology and planting advice was shared and where views were exchanged on current events as well as farm related matters.

Our Fair goes back to a decision made by the New York State Agricultural Society in 1840 to establish an event to address traditional fair interests but on a state-wide basis.

The site of the first ever State Fair, held in Syracuse in 1841, at Salina and Ash Streets. It had a budget of $8,000. Although the weather for it was not great, with an attendance of 10,000 to 15,000, this Fair was labeled a success.

The first Fair was held in Syracuse (then the "Village of Syracuse") in 1841, at Salina and Ash Streets. The location of this annual Fair rotated to various cities in the state thereafter. The first Fair for which admission was charged was held in Rochester in 1843 inside a fenced area (estimated attendance, 20,000). Back in Syracuse in 1849, the Fair was held on James Street Hill (estimated attendance, 65,000). It returned again in early October 1858, held on a 31-acre site east of Onondaga Creek on the South Side of Syracuse (estimated attendance, 80,000). There was one Fair in New York City (in 1854) during these rotations, with low attendance attributed to the difficulty and distance for most to travel there.

With a good option for the purchase of land in the Town of Geddes, and promoted strongly by area leaders, the Fair found its permanent location where it presently stands. It poured rain on opening day, Wednesday, September 11, 1890.

The fairground was originally about 100 acres and early Fair displays and events took place in tents and open fields, with access into and around it on dirt roads.

Attendance grew and bigger crowds came annually to central New York. While successful in drawing crowds to the Syracuse area at the end of the summer, enterprising local business people realized another opportunity. A lack of electricity on the grounds caused the Fair to have to close by nightfall, leaving a need to provide evening entertainment for

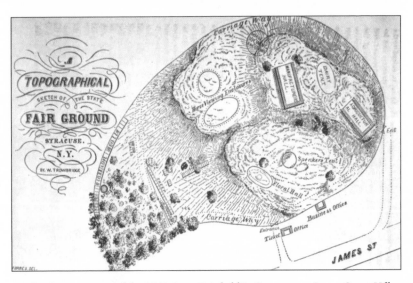

A sketch-map image of the 1849 State Fair held in Syracuse on James Street Hill.

A view of the 1849 State Fair. An admission fee was charged.

the many visitors into the area. So, beginning in 1905, the City of Syracuse began to host an event called the Ka-Noo-No Karnival.

The Karnival was the creation of a group calling itself the Mystic Krew, which claimed to be made up of representatives of the five Indian Nations. The festivities were complete with a parade that contained floats of some degree of design and other events. It quickly came to be referred to as "the Mardi Gras of the northeast." Held in Clinton Square, the Karnival continued until about 1915 and was resurrected for a brief time beginning in 1919, after World War I.

The Fair continued during World War I, even though the grounds also served as a base for training and housing Army recruits. From 1908 through 1937, about 19 permanent structures were built to enhance the fairgrounds and to accommodate to exhibits and competitions. Paved roadways and other improvements were added. The Fair was not held from 1942 through 1947, during World War II – when the grounds were again used as an Army materiel and munitions depot and training area. (See the chapter on Events.)

After World War II, there was some discussion about changing the location of the Fair or not holding it at all, because of the deterioration of the buildings and facilities at the fairgrounds and concerns that the change of the area economy might diminish the general interest in the Fair. As a trial, a five-day Fair was held in 1948, focused mainly on agriculture. The turnout for it (estimated attendance, 25,529) resolved that the Fair was to continue, and at the same location, with State money allocated for facility improvements. Record traffic and crowds for the 1949 Fair (attendance, 355,638) confirmed the decision was a good one.

For a long time, parking took place on the Fair grounds, predominantly on the infield. In more recent years, an abundance of parking has been made available near the fairgrounds. Much of it is on what were the Solvay Process waste beds, with shuttle busses and walkways directly to the fairgrounds. Other parking areas are provided by local businesses and organizations, only a short walk away over Bridge Street. From the earliest days, people more familiar with the area have also found parking in nearby Solvay, walking the distance to the Fair and back.

Over time, the number of Fair days has increased and certain scheduled events have changed. The big race ending the Fair used to take place on the Saturday after Labor Day. But when it became clear that children were missing school to be at the Fair, scheduling of the Fair shifted to end on Labor Day, *before* the regular start of the school year. Admission fees have been low, and have increased gently over time. At the same time, special "days" have been added to the Fair that allow free entry of identified groups – such as students, senior citizens and Veterans. And with all that ease of admission, people *still* sneak into the Fair.

In more recent years, the fairgrounds have been the home of events year-round, making additional use of the property. Buildings were added, with a present accumulation of about 107 permanent structures. The fairground now covers 375 acres. Access to the grounds has improved, in particular because of Rt 690.

Innovations have been and are regularly introduced at the Fair. Small wonder, then, that the first Ferris Wheel was put into place at the 1849 Fair. As with most fairs over time, one could usually find a race track with certain keen interests established on the outcome of those races. (More about that in the chapter on Races.) Also, since its earliest days the Fair has been a place for presidents to visit, politicians to campaign and all levels of society to meet. (See the chapters on People and Special Visitors.)

Some things change, some things remain the same. So it is with the Great New York State Fair.

Note: Credit for the accumulation of a great deal of State Fair history used in this book goes to Henry W. Schramm who produced **A History of the New York State Fair** (North Country Books, Inc.) in 1985. Other information sources include past publications of the Agriculture Society and its proceedings, newspaper reports, the archives of area museums and books cited in the captions of some pictures throughout this book.

The cover from the official program of the Ka-Noo-No Karnival and New York State Fair, 1915. PC

Signs of the Fair

❖•❖

A souvenir post card from the 1907 Fair. PC

★ Having grown up in Lakeland, in addition to the Fair bringing the excitement that hung in the air and meaning the last week of summer vacation, the Fair held particular importance to me. It meant a steady line of traffic that inched along State Fair Boulevard, which in turn meant the boom in business for those along that strip. That included Cerlo's Restaurant, which was owned and operated by my parents, Don and Nickie (Lombard) Cerio. It also meant that for one day Dad would close the restaurant and he and Mom would spend that day with me at the Fair. By that last week of summer vacation I counted the moments leading to our special outing. **K.C. Cerio Bechard**

★ In 1999, I interviewed Bill Fredericks, the full time property manager of the Fair – he's been with the grounds since about 1979. Knows the insides of the fairgrounds pretty well. Knows the seasons of the year, marked by the coming and going of the Fair, it seems. That year, I asked him how he knew when the Fair's ready to start. Told me it had already happened, coming in I-690 that morning. He drove behind a truck hauling cages of chickens. Clouds of feathers swirled over Bill's car and he knew Fair-week had arrived. *Dick Case*

★ It was after the war (World War II), and my parents, Beverly and Rip Ladd, decided to go to the Fair. They were just dating at the time. They drove down Route 11 and to Hiawatha Boulevard. On Hiawatha, near the railroad tracks and the bridge over the Onondaga Creek entrance into the lake, the line of traffic was backed up all the way from the fairgrounds. After crawling along at a snail's pace, they decided to turn around, circle Onondaga Lake and park on the other side of the Fair, figuring no one else had thought of that idea. It took another 30 minutes or so to drive around the lake. Trying to enter from the opposite direction, they found the traffic was just as backed up. My folks ended up parking their car on the side of the road and walked about a mile to get to the entrance to the Fair. They were tired, but once rested, they had an enjoyable day. I'm so glad that the Fair has ample parking lots now to accommodate all the visitors. *Jill Ladd*

★ In the `30s, we knew the Fair was "on" when a large balloon was lofted. The balloon was large, maybe helium-filled, and orange-colored. *Arthur Tindall*

★ During the summer of 1956 I was a flagman at a road construction site off Hiawatha Boulevard. I didn't realize exactly what was being built – eventually it would become Route 690 along the west shore of Onondaga Lake – or how our road work would affect traffic to that year's State Fair. What happened was a detour that re-routed Fair-bound cars from Hiawatha Boulevard to Milton Ave in Solvay, creating perhaps the worst traffic jam in Village history.

The traffic problem even spilled over to where I lived on Russet Lane, our one-block, dead-end street off Orchard Rd, just up the hill from Milton Ave in the Village of Solvay. I sat on our front porch on that Labor Day weekend and watched driver after driver speed up our street, then make an angry, but embarrassed retreat back to Orchard Rd. All the cars had to have been driven by people unfamiliar with Solvay, people who thought they could somehow go around the traffic jam. Some of these people gave up and returned to Milton via Orchard; others circled around via Woods Rd, but that route soon had its own traffic jam.

It was a one-year phenomenon. A year later all roads to the Fair were open and traffic was back to normal on Milton Ave – heavy at times, but moving. *Jack Major*

Note: In 1916, then Lieutenant Governor Edward Schoeneck officially opened what was called a "new, rapid way to the Fair by car", that we call State Fair Boulevard.

★   Some of my earliest memories of the State Fair date back to the early 1930s. My family lived on State Fair Boulevard, near West Genesee St, before Rt 690 was made. As Fair time approached, many performers, horses and other animals would head toward the Fair, right in front of our house. It became a big parade – fun to watch. *Beverly Davis*

★   It was 1949, I think, and the first or one of the first Fairs after World War II. I was living on the south side of Syracuse and decided to go there with my sister Anne and my wife (Carol, who was about seven months pregnant at the time). My brother George volunteered to drive us there. Well, the interest in the Fair was demonstrated by the worst traffic jam ever, with cars bumper-to-bumper and people leaving their cars. When we got to the Fair, we were starved, but it seems that the food supplies had also gotten caught up in the traffic. By that evening we had made our way to a restaurant off the Fair grounds toward Lakeland, ate, and I called my brother to come pick us up. He told me he had just gotten home from dropping us off. *Karl Moberg*

★   My family, the Burton's, started going to the State Fair back as far as I can remember. My Dad, Mom and about nine of us children would head out for a day at the Fair, every year. One year back in the `60s, oh about 1966 (I was six years old and my sister was five), my sister got left behind at the Fair. We had a big van with no seats in the back that we would all pile in at the end of the day and my parents would tell us all to count ourselves. It seems that someone counted themselves twice and my parents didn't notice until we got home. Back they went. Us children ranged in age from three to ten years old, so it was easy to happen. *Shamone Burton*

★ In my job overseeing the physical plant of the fairgrounds, I also handle parking for the Fair. Of course, not everyone can park right next to the entry. My best advice on good parking? You won't believe me when I tell you it's the lot closest to the lake, across from the Fair. I know, it's like telling you to "park the farthest away, and you'll like it", but it happens to be true. Look, you can get there in minutes on a Fair shuttle bus and onto `690 directly from the lot and avoid much of the traffic leaving other parking areas. As to road congestion traffic to the Fair, if it didn't beat all when during a recent Fair I got a telephone call in my office from some woman stuck in traffic who "road raged" me from her car. **Bill Fredericks**

★ Each year the Fair opens with a ribbon cutting ceremony. Each year, the ribbon is cut with a huge, gold-toned pair of ceremonial scissors. I am in charge of graphics and signage at the Fair, have been for years. When that ceremony approaches, sometimes it's a last minute dash – by yours truly – when someone looks up (usually me) and points out that they'll be needing those scissors soon (like that same day). Fortunately, I have a direct connection to the scissor-owner. Those scissors come to the Fair annually borrowed from County Executive Nick Pirro. **Nick Pirro, Jr.**

A recent aerial view of the Fair with the Midway in about the center of the image. SF

Admissions

❧·❦

★ My brothers, sister and I grew up on Seventh St and Cogswell in Solvay. If we wanted to walk down to the Fair, all we had to do was tell our parents and be sure to be home for dinner at 5:00. One day, in about the mid-1970s, my brother Nick called home about 4:45 p.m. He said he was at a friend's house on Power St (only a block away) and asked our mother if he could go to the Fair. After some bargaining, Mom did not relent about being home for dinner. She told Nick to be home in five minutes. There was a short pause on the other end of the line, after which Nick said that he could not get home right away. Mom asked, "Why not?" Nick replied sheepishly, "I'm already at the Fair". It was a while before Nick could leave the house, let alone go back to the Fair. *Dan Petrella*

From the 1931 Fair, Press Grandstand and Press General Admission tickets. PC

★ In about 1923, at the age of ten, our father – Corky (Patrick) Caselle – worked at the restaurant owned by Buttes Mathews. Mr. Mathews, Dad said, was always generous to him. At Fair-time that year he gave Dad a special pass

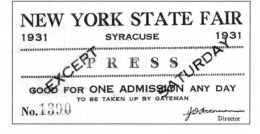

for the Grandstand. Then on Saturday, when the car races took place, he went there with his "gang" of friends. He'd go in, and then put the pass into a Cracker-Jack box after he got in the Grandstand. From there, he'd throw box and with pass inside, down to each one of his gang, until they all got in. *Charmaine Caselle Caffrey* and *Kristen Caselle Klein*

★   In the mid-1920s, when I was about 9 or 10 years old we went to the Fair in bunches. A whole gang of us from Mountain Top in Solvay would walk to the Fair, carrying our packed lunches and we'd walk home again at night. This was an every day happening. We used to crawl under the fence in the back of the fairgrounds by the railroad tracks. One day a State Trooper held the wire fence up for us to crawl under. Most kids skipped school. It got so that the school officials decided not to start school until after the Fair was over. *Frances Wall O'Neil*

★   Back into the 1930s, a big plus about the Fair was the free ticket that was included in everyone's final report card. *Beverly Davis*

★   In the early 1950s, I was fortunate to have a friend who traveled with the James E. Strates Shows. He rented all of the vendor spaces on the grounds and then leased them to other vendors. He became very wealthy doing this. We had free passes to all the sideshows and ate all the popcorn, ice cream, candy apples, and cotton candy we wanted. The nicest experience was meeting all of the Side Show people and my friend's wife, a former *hoochie coochie* dancer. *Thomas R. Demperio*

★   Until 1998, the year I learned about Senior Citizens' Day, I paid little attention to whose "day" it was at the Fair. As of that year, I had not yet earned admission into the AARP (who invite you to join at age 50), but I did have a streak of white at the front of my chin-length hair.
My husband dropped me off at the Main Gate. Armed with my ticket, I walked to the turnstile and presented it to a maybe not quite 20 year-old ticket-taker. "Never mind. Just com'on through," he told me, motioning. "What?" I asked, "Why?" Patiently he explained to me, "It's Senior Citizens' Day, lady. Its free for you." Well, as nice as a free admission might have been, being in non-senior status felt better. I presented my ticket before entering.
This is not to say that as a Solvay child I did not find free entry into

the Fair, but that entry was a "rite of passage" of a different sort. You see, I was let in through the hole in the fence just at the end of the old Bridge Street bridge by my brother Frank. I was probably ten years old, making him twelve-ish. His sharing of this "secret" with me was a badge of "big brother" acceptance. *Judith LaManna Rivette*

★ While working Security at Gate 4 during the Fair, I was approached by a gentleman asking the whereabouts of a former ticket-taker. I told him that the ticket-taker had not been around for some four years. He replied that he was a great friend of the former ticket-taker, who always allowed him entry into the Fair. "Great friend," I repeated. Then I told the man that the reason the former ticket-taker no longer worked was that he had passed away some four years earlier. Without another word, the man retreated and was last seen heading toward the parking lots. *Joe Klodzen*

★ Back in the `30s, we would some times sneak into the Fair, even when we had passes, because it was shorter and quicker than walking around to the main gate. *Arthur Tindall*

★ In the late `40s and `50s, our gang from South Ave would "attend" the State Fair every day, starting by dodging railroad police and sneaking in through a small hole dug dog-like under the big iron fence. We stayed all day and night, subsisting nicely on free samples of fruit, bread, cheese, milk, fruit juice, even meat, I think. (Yardsticks were also a staple.) Entertainment included watching the girls near the small State Trooper building by the fence, listening to the barkers on the Midway and spying on the strippers through holes cut in their dressing room tent. As kids, we never spent any money. *Bob Kanasola*

★ There are a million stories about sneaking into the Fair, especially through the hole in the fence over near Bridge St. At the Fair, some of us actually call that way in the "Solvay Gate." *Bill Fredericks*

★ There are ways of getting free admissions for events at the Fair, and then there are ways of getting free admissions. My way in – actually to the Demolition Derby – was concocted by my friends with one of the volunteer fire departments and was definitely creative. It was also supposed to be smooth, but ended up with a huge amount of notice.

From the 1988 Fair, the Demolition Derby. PHOTO BY STACEY MILLER

The Demolition Derby was required to have a fire truck nearby and it had to be in place before the race could start. My volunteer firefighter friends had entry onto the Fair grounds by driving their truck in, no questions asked, and with only a glance in to see that the passengers were minimal and might, by their dress, be there for fire safety purposes. No one looked on top of the truck. So that's where they planted me, lying down.

All would have worked well, but the truck was unexpectedly called to duty to handle a minor fire on the grounds. I stayed on top. The race was delayed, waiting for the truck. The delay left the race announcer with time on his hands, so he began a play-by-play of the pending arrival of the fire truck. I was still on top. Eventually, the truck moved from the extinguished fire and, amid much attention, to race area. The entire Grandstand watched its approach – and me, still lying across the top of the truck. ***Francis R. Rivette***

★ When we were kids (in the early `60s) and it got to be Fair week, we used to stay overnight at my cousin's house on Horan Rd. The area is back-to-back with the fairgrounds, near the horse barns. What we'd do is cut a hole in the fence and dig a hole under it, sneak in and cover up the hole with brush. Except, we weren't too smart. We wouldn't cover it on both sides. Sure, the State Troopers figured it out and caught us. When they did, the Troopers would pull us by the collar into the horse barns, hand us a shovel, and tell us we had to clean out the manure as punishment. Once they had us – shovel in hand and shaking in our shoes – they'd chase us out telling us not to sneak in, ever again. ***Jake Jakowski***

My aunt and uncle, Rose and Charlie Monti, worked the breakfast shift at the Solvay Tigers stand every year during the Fair. My aunt always chatted with the Midway workers who came in for breakfast. One day when we went to the Fair to meet Aunt Ro-Ro, she had a whole roll of tickets that one of the Midway workers had given her for free. All of us kids had an awesome time at the Fair that year, riding rides all day long with that roll of tickets. *Karen Nicolini Romano*

★ As a young girl (in the `30s or so), we would walk to the Fair and sometimes we would sneak in through a hole in a fence. The Fair was patrolled by NY State Troopers, whom I thought were chosen because they were tall and handsome. I liked them because they would turn their backs to us and make us believe they didn't see us come through under the fence. *Mayola Willoughby*

Note: Until after World War II, there was a minimum height requirement for State Troopers of 6 feet.

★ Jimmy O'Leary and I went to the State Fair early one morning – this would have been in about 1933 or `35 or so – and we stayed there all day. Come at night and time to leave and we decided to stick around. We went into the cow barn and found two empty stalls. They had nice clean hay in them and no cows, so we laid down in the hay. Jimmy fell right asleep. Right away. Well, I didn't.

A little while later, a State Trooper came around and asked what we were doing there. I answered that we were sleeping, but the Trooper wanted to know if we had any cows there. When I told him no (all the while Jimmy was sleeping), he asked where we lived. "We live in Solvay," I answered.

The Trooper kicked Jimmy's foot a few times and finally woke him by gingerly picking him up by the overall straps with a pitch fork. He told us to go with him. In the car he asked again where we lived and I clarified we lived in *East* Solvay. He drove over Bridge St with us in the car and when he got to Milton Ave, he turned right. "That's the wrong way," I told him, "I said we live in East Solvay."

We got a trip with the Trooper that night, all the way to the end of Milton Ave near Onondaga Road, where he let us out, unsympathetic to our protest that it was a long way back from there to home. That was the last time we tried to sleep at the Fair grounds, though. *Robert Doran*

President Clinton at the 1999 Fair, when he visited with First Lady Hillary Clinton. Their motorcade stopped directly in front of the Dairy Building. PHOTO BY SUSAN TACY OSTUNI

★ For Solvay children, entry to the State Fair through a hole in the fence was an end-of-summer windfall. As an adult I found free access to the Fair via other loopholes: as an Assistant District Attorney we volunteered to staff the prosecutor's Fair office, giving us admission and infield parking to compensate us for the after-hours duty; as an Assistant NYS Attorney General, I had to attend the Fair to explain the mission of our office; and in the years when I was a candidate for elected office, attendance at the Comptroller's Day luncheon was required and complimentary admission tickets abounded in political circles.

Many years after my active roll in partisan politics ended, I continued to receive invitations to attend the annual Comptroller's Day Luncheon. Each invite included two complimentary Fair admissions and a free meal. The events were always tame affairs: old political friends greeted each other while candidates for the fall elections "worked the room." The food was always pleasant, but not memorable. The same could be said for the Comptroller's speeches. Obvious from the numerous, vacant place settings, free access to the Fair by this mode did not attract all who were invited.

It was to attend yet another Comptroller's Day Luncheon that I set out for the Fair on a sunny morning, August 30, 1999. A friend offered me a ride, after hearing news reports the parking lots would be full. Unlike previous years, everyone invited was expected to attend the luncheon and those not invited worked all the angles to find that proverbial "hole in the fence." The reason? President Bill Clinton and First Lady Hillary had also accepted the Comptroller's invitation for the free lunch.

This announced visit to the Fair set off the instinctive response – for most of us – that the chance for a close encounter with *the* President would be a once in a lifetime experience.

This became obvious while driving west on Rt 690 that morning, at about three miles before the first Fair exit, when the highway became a parking lot. By 11:00 a.m., we had barely moved along and I needed to reach the main Fair gate by noon, so I asked to be let out of the car and walked the final two miles. The NYS Trooper directing traffic at the exit ramp was not pleased with me, there being an ordinance (he explained) prohibiting walking on the shoulder of a limited access highway. He did empathize with my plea about "the free lunch perk" and sent me on my way. Triumphantly, I presented my invitation at the Fair gate and reached the Empire Court with ten minutes to spare.

Security for entry to the Empire Room was tight, even by today's airport standards. The number of place settings had doubled from past years. After everyone arrived, we were told that Secret Service protocols would require us to remain in the room after the President entered and until he left. Even urgent rest room visits would be discouraged.

Enter the President and First Lady. Everyone seemed awed by the glow of his Presidential aura. As was Bill Clinton's special gift, he immediately connected with his audience by remarking: "Teddy and Taft may have been the first, but I bet I've been to more State Fairs. I've never met a State Fair I didn't like." In that moment I thought to myself, "Isn't that the truth?" *Tony Gigliotti*

Competitions

From the **Transactions of the N.Y. State Agricultural Society, 1859,** *this is an engraved illustration showing "Prince of Oxford". The caption reads "a prize winning Red Roan that won first prize at the New York Agricultural Society's Show at Syracuse, 1858, as the best Short Horn Bull, one year old."* CONTRIBUTED BY BARBARA S. RIVETTE.

★ With my mother's permission, I went to the New York State Fair at age ten for a whole week in 1935. My Milking Shorthorn heifer, Clover Queen, had been considered good enough to compete in the 4-H show at the State Fair. I was to be "looked after" by the Monroe County 4-H summer assistant, a Cornell senior student.

Being "looked after" consisted of making sure I had my heifer cared for, that she was ready for showing and asking me if everything was okay. For the rest of the time, I wandered the Fair, made many friends and missed very little of the many exhibits, shows and excitements. As a protected boy from an isolated farm, I was excited about all the things that I was seeing.

Along with other 4-H exhibitors (most of whom were older) I bunked in the Pyrke Youth Building, with meals in the building cafeteria. The 4-H barn was brand new that year and dedication ceremonies were conducted midweek by Governor Herbert H. Lehman.

My heifer won several blue and purple ribbons and was judged the Grand Champion of the Milking Shorthorn breed, both 4-H and open class.

This wonderful experience, for a whole week at age ten, started a life-long friendship with fairs in general and the State Fair in particular. During the intervening seventy years, and having become a Doctor of Veterinary Medicine, I have been involved with the Fair in many ways and I still try to help make sure that the Fair will bring excitement and a happy experience to boys and girls of all ages. ***Bruce Widger***

★   My second most memorable NY State Fair visit – after meeting my husband there in 1951 – was 44 years later. That was when our 10-year-old granddaughter modeled in a fashion show on the stage in the Woman's Building. What a proud grandmother I was. ***Gail Draper***

★   In 1960 our family started showing Shorthorn Beef Cattle at the New York State Fair. At that time we were housed in the big stone barn now used by horses. We had our tie-out area outside the fence along the railroad tracks. In 1965, we tied all cattle out at night. During the night someone decided to cut the ropes that held the cattle and all the exhibitors were very glad that the cattle stayed where they were tied. In 1989 the Beef Cattle were moved to a new pole barn during that Fair season. The first day of that Fair, it was 26°, with the wind blowing. The water in the buckets froze, so we had to break the ice to water cattle. We considered this a welcome to our new barn. ***Thomas G. Patton***

★   One year I performed in a piano recital at the then-called Women's Building, on what had to be a 100° day. I was very nervous (not to mention very hot), but what kept me going was knowing that my reward for a job well done was to be able to spend the rest of the day at the Fair. (I don't think that a recital could have gone any slower.) ***Heather Brady***

From the 1891 Fair, the second Fair held in its present permanent location, this ribbon awarded "Best Stallion of Any Age". The original is about 13" long and carries the seal of the New York State Agricultural Society. PC

★   The New York State Fair was so much a part of my life growing up in Solvay. It was the yearly indicator pointing to the official end of summer and beginning of the school year.

My special memories of the Fair include watching my grandmother, Jessie Baratta, practice and prepare for the baking competition in the Women's Building. She was required to submit a written recipe and a freshly baked entry the morning of the competition, with a choice of entries each day. The Best of the Fair, Grand Prize competition was on Labor Day. Many a morning Grandma would get up very early and bake several recipes before she was satisfied with the one deemed worthy to compete. Off we would go with her baked goods, our special parking sticker and our exhibitor passes. We would drop off her entries, go see the other sights of the Fair and return often to see if the judging was complete.

As a young child, I felt pretty important to be a part of such an event. Sometimes, Grandma and I would stand in front of the judge's booth (open for public view) and watch as they critiqued every aspect of a pie, cake or cookies. The cookie size had to be uniform, the color of a pie crust had to be golden, the texture of a cake had to have a fine crumb and of course, the taste had to be outstanding.

We couldn't get close enough to hear the judges' comments, but my grandmother would try to guess their opinions by watching their facial expressions or their desire to try "second helpings". Sometimes she would make not-so-positive comments about other peoples' entries and I would try to hush her up for fear they might be standing in the crowd nearby.

My grandmother won countless ribbons for her baking abilities and by the time I was 13-years old she had me hooked on the competition. I learned to bake from the best – Grandma and my mother, Jennie

Wilson. The baking competition was fun and exciting for me and I continued to enter for over 20 years. **Judy Wilson Merritt**

★   For the last five years, I have entered photographs in the NYS Fair photography exhibit. So far, I have received a Second Place ribbon in the amateur competition and both First and Fourth Place ribbons in the Senior Citizen competition. It's pretty exciting – as a number of my photographs have been displayed at the Fair, as well. **Richard C. Lauricella**

4-H Club Member

CAMP PYRKE

New York State Fair

SEPT. 5 TO 12

1931

From the 1931 Fair, a 4-H Club Member Ribbon. PC

★   The State Fair holds many memories for my three children, and to this day, coming home to go to the Fair is a big treat. They all belonged to a 4-H Dairy Club – during the late 1960s and early '70s – so showing their cattle after many months of getting them ready was the highlight of the year. (One of my daughters won Master Showman in the Coliseum ring at the age of twelve – quite an accomplishment.) They had to wear "show whites" to go in the ring with their prize animal, but those "whites" were not white very long. Many's the time, if I was able and available, that I would be the one to rush home to Baldwinsville from the Fair grounds to wash the "whites" and get them back in time for their next show.

The children practically lived in the 4-H barns for the week of the Fair. In showing cattle they soon learned that some win and some don't – a very early learning experience. There was such camaraderie among the 4-H kids, all wanting to win, but happy for those who did if they didn't. And it was great for the parents, as well. We were a whole big family. **Elizabeth Bowers**

★   When we were young, we would take a bag lunch to the Fair, to eat in the Coliseum where there was judging of cattle. In about the '30s, John Luchsinger, treasurer of the Solvay school system, was one of the judges. **Mayola Willoughby**

★ On August 27, 1968, I sat in a hot, stuffy room at the Art and Home Center, awaiting my turn as a contestant in the New York State Fair Spelling Bee. I was invited because I'd finished eighth in the Herald American Spelling Bee earlier that year. The invitation to the Fair gave me a second chance to prove how good a speller I was. I studied the usual list of difficult words.

The first round of any spelling bee usually consists of easy words, and the Fair's bee was no exception. But when I got to the microphone, I was given an eight-letter word to spell.

I stood in the air-conditioning-challenged auditorium, and began to spell slowly and deliberately, as usual. I got the first five letters out with no trouble. Then my brain, apparently unable to cope with such a humid climate, decided to leave me – on a trip (to where I can't be sure), but did reluctantly return to my cranium. My head once again intact, I finished the word. And heard the bell. Turns out that in giving the sixth letter I had repeated the fifth letter, making the eight-letter word a nine-letter one that apparently doesn't exist in any dictionary.

Then things got worse. Although at other bees you got to leave if you missed a word, at the State Fair bee, I wasn't let off the hook quite so easily. Instead, as the last-place finisher (35th out of 35), I had to return to my seat and stay there through the rest of the competition.

Now 37 years have passed, and I've spent most of them as a copy editor at The Post-Standard. My bosses and the reporters tell me that I take special pains to make sure that the stories and the headlines are accurate. (I even was on our team in two corporate spelling bees, one of which we won. So maybe the curse is over.) Still, you'd be interested to know the word that tripped me up back then, the word that I spelled inaccurately. Well, if you must know, that word was: accurate.
Mark Murphy

★ I am a farmer's wife. Each year our children got ready to show the heifers and cows of the farm, with many days of cleaning, grooming and training them for the show ring. And in Spring our family gardening started, to prepare for the 4-H show. Vegetables had to grow just right, to enter, so many nights after school the children also cared for the garden. The girls also sewed for the 4-H fashion show at the Fair. Our daughter had a dog she showed each year in the 4-H ring and a costume show also was fun.

I tell you all this because each year (for about five years) we, the Nelson family, would travel 200 miles to the Fair. This was a way we helped our children grow, by their doing the farm animal shows and the 4-H show. They stayed-over, living at the Fair while we traveled back home. We would come back a day or two later, to see the blue and red ribbons they won. In this work, our children grew in body and mind. They developed and grew up, while at the same time enjoying the State Fair.

Now that they are all grown up, we parents live only twelve miles away from the Fair. We go on Senior Citizen Day, Veterans Days. We travel by bus, which is a short ride for us, now, to attend the State Fair. At the Fair each year we enjoy knowing our children were here once and we remember growing up our children here at the State Fair. *Gladys Nelson*

★ My older sister Tina was in a band with the Mexico High School. We would watch her compete at the Fair, rain or shine. *Shamone Burton*

From the 1973 Fair official program book, the New York State high school marching band competition. Traditionally held on opening day, awarding prize money and trophies for the field show contest and parade competition at the Grandstand. NP

★ One small news article in 1977 led me to years of fun filled times that translated to lasting memories. That article invited local persons who enjoyed cooking and baking to enter their culinary wares in the NYS Fair. "Win or lose," I thought, "that would be a fun thing to do." That year, my oldest daughter (Suzanne – who was about to enter college to study dietetics) and I both entered several items and we were lucky enough to win some ribbons. That was an addiction in the making.

She and I entered together for the next several years, wreaking havoc in the kitchen during that last week of summer. After Sue married and moved away, I continued competing. I enjoyed my friendships with the other regular entrants as much as the thrill of the contest. Many of us only crossed paths that one time each year, but we seemed to have bonded because of our common passion for cooking and respect for the other's talent.

My husband got used to being a guinea pig during that time and gave in to celebrating our August 31st wedding anniversary at the Fair each year. He passed away two years ago but I felt his presence as I entered and won on August 31, 2004. What really made the 2004 Culinary Competition at the Fair especially exciting for me was the winnings by six of my granddaughters, ages 11-14 (Kelsey, Tori and Cali Eckler, Kaitlin Ehland and Michele and Kristen Atkinson).

The girls spent time together at my house creating, baking (and having fun) getting their entries ready for Youth Day. Their efforts resulted in three First Place ribbons, two in Second Place and one placed Third. Kelsey, the youngest, also won the kids Spam contest. Twenty-seven years of fun times competing at the Fair and a card board box full of ribbons couldn't compare to the pride that I felt as I watched them gleefully accept their ribbons. *Phyllis A. Eckler*

★ In 1935 or 1936 my father, Tom Neary, won the trap shoot contest at the Fair breaking 99 out of 100. The prize was a complete hunting outfit. *John Neary*

★ Each year on Labor Day, the New York State Fair hosts the Rooster Crowing Jamboree Championship. The daily winners for the first eleven days of the Fair compete on this last day for the title of Jamboree Champion. These eleven roosters have won their eligible place by crowing more times than any other rooster for the 15 minute counting period.

The Brouillette family has exhibited poultry at the Fair since 1985. It won the Crowing Championship for their first time at the 2004 NYS Fair. The family had entered the show each year and finally had a finalist on the Championship Day (Labor Day), when the Fair was cancelled due to a huge storm the night before. Our winner was a young black Bantam with a strong will to crow, but it never showed again.

The guy who won the most throughout the nineties and early this century was Paul Jones of Oneida with his handsome Game Roosters.

The 2003 Championship came down to the Jones' Game Cock edging out the Brouillette's 8-year old white Polish Rooster by two crows to win the championship. That old White Polish rooster with the genuine spirit passed away that next winter but not before siring three sons: one son hatched bearded, one son hatched non-bearded and the third lost an eye to LT vaccine.

Well, the two roosters grew up to follow Old Whitie's spirit and won the daily contests on the 10th and 11th days in 2004.

The stage was set for Championship Day with the two Brouillette White Polish roosters, three of Jones' Game Cocks and several other fine roosters. The roosters came out of the dark at 11 o'clock sharp to begin the crowing contest. The crowd gathered to cheer-on their favorites. Mr. Jones paced nervously keeping his eyes on the roosters and tally cards. However, this time Whitie's bearded son edged out the Jones Gamecock by two crows, for a win. *Karen and Rudy Brouillette*

This quilt motif Fair poster has been one of the most popular created by the Fair. JPL

★ The tour of the Fair with my mother Joanne started at the Women's Building, where we were greeted with rich colors of tapestry suspended around the perimeter, yielding to yet more artistic skill within – tatted lace, knit and sewn items. Proud I was to see there, among the rest, my entry – a dainty, crocheted christening gown – that had won a blue ribbon. *Brenda Lotito*

★ Probably in the `60s, when I was by then an artist-member of the Associated Artists, I was standing at the entrance to the Art Exhibit at the Fair. I remember that

Governor Rockefeller was touring the exhibit. My old art teacher came by and paused for a moment to say to me, "Bette, what in the world are you doing here?" And I answered with becoming modesty, "One of my paintings is in the exhibit inside." You see, when I was a senior at Eastwood High School, that same teacher (I can't recall her name) looked at my diagram of an oval and said firmly, "You'll never get anywhere, Bette. You can't even draw a straight line." Well, I've painted every day since, sold a few paintings and then decided it was too much like selling my children. I am now 85 years old. **Bette Hughes Killecut**

A competition sheep. SF

★ My love of sheep and shepherding brought me to the New York State Fair for the first time in 1976 and two years later I brought sheep to show at the Fair. Feeling like a fledgling 4-H-er, I slept – and not very well – on a cot in a pen adjacent to my sheep. To my delight my first time there, a lamb I entered in the Carcass Class was awarded a Grand Champion ribbon. **Millie Bankert**

Exhibits

✦•❦

★ My association with the New York State Fair is that for many years I have demonstrated the use of old woodworking tools. I am usually found outside of the Agriculture Museum. Some people say that I look like Santa Claus because of my long white beard and my ... er ... size. I weigh-in at about 220 pounds. (Hence my nickname of Nick). In my demonstrations, I often use a question and answer format to make the presentation more interesting.

One time I had just completed showing some children how to make and assemble the components for a small stepstool from a tree. Then I questioned the audience to see if they could figure what the seat would be

From the 1996 Fair, antique tool user and storyteller William "Nick" Nichols, who gives daily woodworking demonstrations in front of the Witter Agriculture Museum. SF

made of. Some guesses were good. "Cattails?" offered one youngster, to which I replied, "Doesn't that make the cats mad?"

Then I explain that the seat is made from a product called paper rush, basically brown Kraft paper (as used in paper grocery bags). The paper is twisted into a cord and then woven into a seat on the frame. To demonstrate how strong the seat is, I stood right in the middle of the stool on one foot and pointed out, "It's just paper," adding, "Isn't that amazing?" A little girl replied, "You cheated." I asked her "How's that?" She said, "You only stood on *one* foot." (I tried it on the bathroom scales. It doesn't work that way.) **Nick (William) Nichols**

★   A favorite exhibit of mine and many in the 1930s or so, was the dog trials (retrievers) at the pool. Those are gone now. **Beverly Davis**

★   Probably everyone's earliest Fair memory is the large ear of corn in the Indian Village. As a child I thought it was as tall as a skyscraper. We have a picture of my sister, brother and I standing in front of it. In later years, I took a picture of my children standing in front of it, too. **Charmaine Caselle Caffrey**

★   One of my earliest State Fair memories is of an eager little goat who snatched my bright orange Lost Kid Tag right off my belt loop at the petting zoo. (From that point on, I truly believed that goats ate anything.) **Heather Brady**

★   During Wayne Gallagher's tenure as Director, I worked as Entry Coordinator. My job was to oversee the processing of thousands of entries, from dogs, horses, cakes, paintings and cattle. My favorite part

From the 1994 Fair, Cinderella (Christa Salmon) and her coach at one of the daily afternoon parades. PHOTO BY MARY ELLEN DAINO

of the job was seeing the looks on children's faces when they received their coveted Blue Ribbon. At this same time I was the Parade Coordinator of the Fair's daily parade. Our Entry Department staff would dress up each day to participate, including our families. One year, my daughter Libby dressed up as Cinderella and rode in the Commerford Pumpkin Carriage; another year she was Little Bo Peep and her sister was Humpty Dumpty. **Mary Ellen Daino**

★ My father was a member of the Grange and I belonged to 4-H, this was in the `60s as I recall. My five brothers and I – we grew up on a farm in Central Square – would be so excited to see all the Fair exhibits, especially those having to do with farming such as the tractors and big machinery. I most enjoyed going to the Coliseum and watching the horse shows. We walked through every single animal barn there. The smells were so very interesting. Once, we bought a Hereford Bull that I knew had been to the State Fair because he smelled like the Fair. Of course, I was only about eleven or twelve years old at the time, so what did I know? **Jill Ladd**

★ There were baby bunnies at the Fair, all fuzzy and adorable. And, as usual, we petted and rubbed noses with numerous friendly furballs. One of the bunnies found my wife's cow-spotted Texas hat as Laura bent over to look closely at the seemingly sedate bunny. The little rascal snatched that hat up with his teeth and yanked it right off her head. She had quite a wrestling match with the "mad hatter" to get it back, with onlookers enjoying the "woman wrestles rabbit" event. **Ted Rozelsky**

★ My favorites from the early years of the Fair ranged from the gigantic colored-paper parasol flowers and the dog-less harnesses to the "slide for life" exhibit at the military display located at Miller Court. I remember seeing Gomer Pyle belt out "God Bless America" and seeing other musical celebrities there. We would leave after the free concert in Miller Court. **Catherine Savo**

★ I've been showing my beef cattle at the State Fair since age ten, when I became old enough to compete in the 4-H show. Now I'm 14 and still showing my beef cattle along with dairy cattle and dairy goats. Last year, I arrived at the Fair with my dairy cattle and goats on

August 25, 2004. I was going to unload my dairy cattle first and then my goats, but my plans sort of changed. I had been waiting for a long time to get them checked-in when someone told me that there was a problem. The Veterinarians who were making the inspections saw some sores on some other animals' mouths, and suspected hoof and mouth disease. Samples were sent to New York City on a helicopter for testing.

The Superintendent called a meeting and told us we were quarantined. The animals already there could not leave the fairgrounds or even the barn. It was very scary. I then unloaded my dairy cattle and goats. My goats and I had to stay in the dairy cattle barn until the results came back, so I had to put them in a pen in Moo Country. The next morning at about 3:00 a.m. we got the news that the animals were negative for hoof and mouth disease and everyone was so glad. I went to the goat barn to have my friends come back and help me bring my goats and stuff down. I was so relieved. That was a very exciting start to my 2004 NYS Fair. I will never forget that year. *Gabrielle Glenister*

From the 1994 Fair, veterinary surgery being performed at the Horse Barn. ꜱꜰ

★ When my brother Jim and I were just little kids, my Mom would take us to the Fair early in the morning to avoid the crowds. This really was the best time of day to experience the various animals, because there was so much activity in the agricultural buildings. On one occasion, we were fortunate enough to arrive in the cow barn just moments after the birth of a brand new calf. Eyes as big as saucers of milk, my brother and I stared at the placenta hanging from the cow. "Mom, I ain't never gonna drink milk no more," my brother, all of five, uttered as he twisted his face in disgust and walked away. *Catherine LaManna*

★ The 1876 log cabin in the Witter Museum is a focal exhibit, furnished with period pieces. Everything one would find inside of a log cabin. It is a pretty popular spot. But we didn't realize how inviting it was until one night, just before closing the building. That's when we discovered that a visitor had slipped into the log cabin and – just like Goldilocks – was sleeping on the rope bed. *Millie Bankert*

★ I love to go to the Fair. One of my favorite times of going to the Fair was last year because the tigers were there. I think that there were about three big tigers and two little tigers. The little tigers rolled around and played with a ball. They were adorable. The big tigers were relaxing, lying in the sun, and they were beautiful. *Amy Ruszczak*

From the 2004 Fair, the butter sculpture "viewed" by Jeremy Hanlon. SF

★ One job I held briefly was working for a local advertising agency that had the American Dairy Association and Dairy Council of New York as one of its accounts. For the Fair, I worked on the support staff, helping set up the area promoting New York's dairy industry. It was hot work at the Fair, but at least we had the advantage that we could slip in to "inspect progress" on the butter sculpture in its refrigerated splendor – but not very often. The sculptor had a very firm view on how often the access door could be opened, as it had an effect on his concentration. *Barbara Lucas*

★ The butter sculpture, a traditional exhibit at the New York State Fair, is displayed inside a glass case in which the butter is kept cold. For most, it is an experience to see. For the visually impaired, like me, for whom touch is a way to experience the world, the sculpture has not been viewable. Going to the Fair from when I was ten year old, I always wondered what the butter sculpture *looked* like. I wanted to jump inside that cooler to find out. When I was 13-years old, I remember walking away from the butter sculpture in tears, frustrated from every-one's attempts to describe that year's sculpture to me, feeling so left out. I am now almost 20 years old.

For a few years I tried a write-in campaign to the Fair, to suggest they display a touchable replica near to the butter sculpture for the visu-ally impaired, but nothing happened.

Fast-forward to 2003, when, in the course of working an internship with local radio station and NPR affiliate WRVO, I was the interviewer for a story about what a blind person would encounter while going to the Fair. At the butter sculpture, I asked a gentleman (identified as an Army Veteran) what he would recommend to the Fair so the visually impaired could see the sculpture, just like others. He recommended there be a replica displayed for touching.

The story aired and eventually was honored with a Press Club Award. At that Press Club Award Dinner a representative from the Fair told me that because of the WRVO story there would be a touchable replica of the butter sculpture at the Fair.

I was still an intern at WRVO in 2004 and we decided to do a fol-low-up to the butter sculpture story. Jim Victor was the sculptor again that year. I was thrilled when they brought the replica to me, more thrilled to learn I was the first blind person to feel the replica. It felt like hard butter.

Just as I was getting ready to leave, Jim Victor invited me into the cooler to touch the real butter sculpture. This was an experience I had thought about since I was ten years old. I put out my right hand onto the butter sculpture, and every question I had about what it felt like, what it looked like – all the wonder – was answered. *Jeremy Hanlon*

★ The first time I went inside the Agricultural Museum at the New York State Fair, I was amazed. I thought it would be boring, but it was anything but boring to me. There was a room that had a wood turning demonstration. A man there was making a broom. An old-fashioned cabin was on display. A lady was weaving cloth on a loom. We saw many horse carriages and we learned about flax. It was fun – a lot of fun. *Seth Randall*

★ In the Sheep and Swine Building, one of the swine pens had the sides covered with burlap bags, so you could not see into the pen without stepping on a stool. Next to the stool was a big sign reading "See the Green Pig." A big line would form to see the green pig. When you stepped onto the stool and looked in you saw yourself reflected in a big mirror. *John Neary*

★ In 1972 I was asked by the Aviation Historical Society to display my 1931 *Tiger Moth* Biplane in the Center of Progress building at the Fair. I flew the plane in, landed in the lower parking lot and towed it by truck to the Center of Progress Building. We suspended it from the ceiling in the NASA wing. It was displayed all of Fair week that year. After the Fair was over, we towed the plane back to the lower parking lot and left from there. We took off to the delight of the traffic stopped on Rt 690. *Dick Forger*

From the 1972 Fair, the 1931 Tiger Moth Biplane on display at the Center of Progress Building. PHOTO BY DICK FORGER

Places

★ State Park of the Fair. It's New York's smallest park – size of three acres. The place really looks like a park, with walkways, grass, trees and picnic tables circling the pool. Some buildings around it – like the Visitor's Center and a Gift Shop. **Dick Case**

★ The Daniel Parris Witter Agriculture Museum, an impressive brick building, sits back from the road and opposite the Coliseum. It houses a collection of agricultural and domestic artifacts and the history of agriculture is presented there through exhibits, interpreters and demonstrations. Visitors frequently enter the building asking, "Is this place new?" My response over the years that I served as its Superintendent, "It was new in 1928."

The State Park at the Fair, located opposite the entrance to the Horticulture Building. JPL

During my tenure as Superintendent, we opened the Witter Museum in the spring and autumn for school children and other visitors, and interpreters and demonstrators help present the last two centuries of agricultural history. The students visiting from the City of Syracuse or other non-rural places were often quite unfamiliar with the ways of agriculture and the country lifestyle. Their surprise when they learned about food products – like just where their "packaged" food comes from and that "corn" provides the sweetener in soft drinks – was delightful. **Millie Bankert**

★   There were some old stables near the race track at the Fair. It seemed – at least to me and my cousin Tom Smolinski – that they that hadn't been used (or more specifically, cleaned) for several years. Our summer job at the fairgrounds was to clean them, which wasn't easy when you work with one hand clamped over your nose to block the odor. *Jack Major*

★   I had some of my first driving lessons at the fairgrounds. Those wide-open spaces were ideal for learning how to drive, especially in the snow. My uncle Bumbalooch (Paul) Mascette or my brother Cabbage (Rich) Nicolini would take me to the fairgrounds for a driving lesson. As I drove along, whoever was with me would reach over with his left foot, slam on the brakes and say, "Now, get out of the skid" and I did. Did anybody else use the fairgrounds for driving lessons? *Karen Nicolini Romano*

★   The Fair meant Lost Kid Tags, chocolate milk (the coldest in town) from the Dairy Building, a spin-art masterpiece, a candy apple, some cotton candy, a pony ride, the bumper cars, and the best thing of all, the Indian Village where each of my yearly visits to the Fair would end. The magic of Indian Village was transforming: the native music, native costumes, native rituals were all awe-inspiring. I would drink-in all the sights and sounds. And when it came time to select my State Fair souvenir, each year I waited for my journey through the Indian Village to pick that special keepsake.

I recently ran across some of my most cherished treasures from those magical Indian Village days: a beaded necklace and a brightly colored, beaded Native American headband with leather ties. At one time I also had a beautifully beaded change purse and rabbit's foot key chains that were meant to bring good luck.

Our tradition of visiting the Indian Village transcended into the next generation: my husband Brian and I always make that our last stop with our two sons Jared and Connor. We share their excitement with the sights; their interest in souvenirs runs a little different from mine (tomahawks, sling shots, bow and arrows, and head dresses). **K.C. Cerio Bechard**

Note: Indian Village was added to the fairgrounds with a dedication ceremony that took place in 1928. A Corn Marathon run – from the Onondaga Reservation to the fairgrounds – was part of the ceremony.

★ Politicians were regular visitors to the New York State Fair and women who were trying to obtain the right to vote in 1911 saw a great opportunity.

One of the ardent women suffrage workers was Harriet May Mills of Syracuse, whose uncle, Henry Mills, owned an early automobile. She persuaded him to let the suffrage leaders use his open car as their speaking platform at the State Fair. It's hard to determine at this late date whether those in the audience were more fascinated with the 1910 right hand drive six-cylinder Franklin car or the message from the elaborately dressed ladies in their large hats the size of bushel baskets.

In 1920, after women obtained the right to vote, Miss Mills was the unsuccessful Democratic candidate for Secretary of State, the first woman to run for a state-wide office on a major party ticket. The Mills Memorial Women's Building at the State Fair was named in her honor and dedicated in 1935, the year of her death. **Barbara S. Rivette**

★ One day, touring the Fair as a newspaper reporter, I went to the Poultry, Pigeon and Rabbit Building to meet its superintendent, John Pierce. The Poultry Building went up in 1913. It's rated the oldest and

From **The New York State Fair: Its Record, Its Character and its Meaning** *by John B. Howe, 1917, an early photo of the duck pond in the interior of the Poultry Building at the Fair.*

CONTRIBUTED BY MARY ELLEN CHESBRO

maybe the largest in the country. The building, along the path to the Midway, is one of the Fair's big destinations. Inside we were greeted with two and a half stories of chorusing animals, fur, feathers and about 2,000 birds in 500 classes.

John's a friendly guy from South Onondaga – a retired industrial arts teacher – who grew up in the hilly farmland around Navarino in the Town of Onondaga. He's been coming to the Poultry, Pigeon and Rabbit Building since he was a kid. "My first job here was sweeping the floor," John explained as we walked around the second-floor balcony above the show area. He opened a door and added, "I slept in this dormitory." The Fair showed a lot more poultry when he started, maybe 8,000 birds back then, and they'd arrive at the Fair in railroad boxcars to the main gate.

The building was breezy and babbly, despite signs warning "No Loud Noise". Folks wandered in and sat around the duck pond at the center of the show floor. Rabbits to the right, pigeons upstairs and someone sold peacock feathers, two for a buck. The Syracuse Racing Pigeon Club had a coop at the front door. A rooster-crowing contest, held each morning in the charge of John Rebhahn – that day had with ten contestants, judged by four volunteers who "counted crows" (the number of crows in 15 minutes).

One other use of the building. The Yankee Fall Classic. A consortium of six New York state poultry clubs helped to bring something like 4,000 birds and 3,000 breeders to the building in October, 2004, for the American Poultry Association's National meet and competition – the first time in Syracuse. **Dick Case**

It was not really part of the Midway, that pony ride. It was way in the back corner of the Fair grounds, mostly away from everything, but my father found it. At the time, like most pre-teenage girls, I was infatuated with horses. I had a small, bronzed-looking horse statuette. I drew horse pictures all the time. I knew about bridles and reins and all. But I had never been *on* one. They were just beautiful creatures to me. Also, I was inspired by my father's interest – he had served in a cavalry division of the Army in World War II. So Daddy found me a pony ride. This had to have been some time in the late `50s. It wasn't much of a location and there was hardly a line to speak of. The ride consisted of maybe four ponies that were walked in circles as you sat on them. You got to pick your pony, and fearlessly, I made my selection. Once on top, the height and movement startled me. Making no big deal about my visible panic, Dad took over the reins of my pony and walked around with me in circle after circle of my first pony ride ever. *Judith LaManna Rivette*

The cover photo, from a post card of the Main Gate entrance of the Fair, undated but probably from the early 1900s. PC

Entertainment

A post card showing "Flying Airships". PC

Note: Air shows and stunt flying was a form of entertainment at the Fair in the early 1900s through about 1920.

★   The Tiger Show is a favorite of Fair-goers, so it is often on the schedule of the sign language interpreters. During the pre-show patter, the trainer pointed to the interpreter beneath the Fair's blue, "Access for the Deaf" flag, noting that she was "within range" in the event a tiger need to relieve himself. Not wanting to become a target, she included an additional message when she interpreted to the deaf audience. "Please," she signed, "if you see the tiger lift his tail, let me know immediately." Another time, it seems that the movements of the sign language interpreter fascinated Minnie the Sea Lion. The trainers were having trouble getting Minnie to focus on their commands, she was so intent on watching the interpreter. Near the end of the show, Minnie got her own laugh. When she emerged from the water at the edge of the tank, she splashed her flippers, showering the interpreter with salt water. *Jim and Cathy Skvorak*

★   One year, when I tuned the piano for Tiny Tim's appearance, I had all of the sound and amplifiers turned off so I could hear to do my tuning. I am – if I do say so – a pretty good impersonator and somewhat of a jokester. So, when I was done tuning, I stood on the stage and sang "Tiptoe, through the tulips" in my best Tiny Tim voice and people came running. "Relax," I told them, "it's just the piano tuner singing." *Kenneth A. Williams*

★   My sister and I once snuck into a girly show at the Fair. I guess we were about 15 and 10-years old. We thought we were seeing and doing something very risky. The show had Barkers who would entice the crowd outside to come into the shows. They would bring out one of the "girls" – always one that was younger and pretty – to give a little demonstration. Inside, the strippers were old, out of shape and not too attractive, but their spangles went a long way to distract from those facts. We thought the show was great. It was extremely tame, compared to today's entertainment standards – more like vaudeville with a comedienne and a magic act. *Kristen Klein*

★   One afternoon in 1938, when I first started working at the Fair, I was going to the ladies' room and I ran into a beautiful girl who had on a Southern Belle dress. She was wearing a great big bonnet, with a huge ribbon on its side. Her name was Gypsy Rose Lee. The same year, Sammy Kay's band played. Another time, Tennessee Ernie Ford was standing in front of my office one morning and Anita Bryant was standing right next to him. They were waiting for someone to pick him up. She hadn't noticed, but he was bleeding on his left cheek. He thanked me when I gave him a tissue and told him to "spit on it" and put it on his shaving nick. Jerry Vail was at the Fair in the `60s, when I was Ticket Manager for all the events at the Fair. One day I found him in front of my office, all alone, looking handsome with his beautiful white hair just so. When I asked him if he needed anything, he replied, "I'm supposed to be a celebrity and not one person that has passed me has recognized me." *Madge Wells*

★ I started clogging when I turned 50 years old. In 1982 my husband Bill and I formed our first group, the Adirondack Mountain Cloggers, which I teach and direct. In 1983 we performed for the first time for the New York State Fair Grange. We also started dancing at the Art and Home Center with our group. I have been clogging and tap dancing at the State Fair for 21 years. I am 77 years old. It has been delightful to see how the Fair grows bigger and bigger each year. *Julia Tourtellotte*

★ You know, all the performers have certain requirements when they come to the Fair and you would not believe the range of demands

BBKing at the 1999 State Fair. sf

– from the very modest (a can of Campbell's Chicken Noodle soup and a pot warmer) to the exotic (black caviar) and including specifications on the color of the towels for them in the dressing room. One stands out – I can't name any names here – that wanted a bushel of pears per day of performance. Most of the entertainers are very gracious. Like, for example, Ann Murray who invited us in back stage to join her for dinner before the show, just like regular folk. *Bill Fredericks*

★ Aahhh. The New York State Fair. The Fair is one of New York's greatest wonders. My favorite memory of the Fair was when I was eight years old. They had hired a guy to ride his unicycle at the Fair and he had to pick someone from the crowd to ride on his shoulders. Lucky me. I raised my hand and was chosen. I've never been more scared in my life. It was very fun, but riding a bike has never been the same after that. *Sandra Simmons*

★ One time I was at the Fair with my parents, sister and brother. This was probably about 1965 and I was 15. We were sitting at the free music court (was it Cole Muffler Court back then?) watching Lyonel

Hampton and his orchestra perform. During one song he invited a few audience members to join him on the stage to dance to his music. I got right up and started doing a go-go type dance on the stage. I'll never forget the look on my parents' faces of shock and amazement that I would do such a thing. *Charmaine Caselle Caffrey*

★ One of the special attractions at the 1996 State Fair was the Musical Ride of the Royal Canadian Mounted Police. State Fair Security was to escort the Mounties, their horses and equipment trucks to the racing stables where they were to be headquartered. We were to meet them at a specific gate and lead them via the easiest route to the stables. Watchful as we were, the Royal Canadians entered the wrong gate and began to make their own way to the stables. I was dispatched to catch up with them and guide them in. I took off in my golf cart on an inside route. Security Officer David "Dapper" Clifford – with a clear view of it all from Gate 9 – offered a play-by-play of my near-misses over his portable two-way radio. I finally caught up with the Mounties at the racing stables, where they had begun unloading.

Many of the Fair's added attractions carry an extra admission fee, but in 1996 the four days of performances of this group at the Coliseum was to be free. A free event to a Fairgrounds full of people and placed in a building with a capacity of approximately 5000 people, including standing room, was a recipe for a distinctly interesting afternoon.

For the first afternoon of the performance, Dick Morgan and I were on Security assigned to the Coliseum. It was hot, brutally hot and humid. Morgan and I were positioned at the main Coliseum entrance facing what is known in the State Fair as Restaurant Row.

The Coliseum filled rapidly. Fairgoers continued to stream in and it became clear we would have to start turning people away. We tried, but had to be assisted in our efforts by a detachment of State Troopers under the command of First Sergeant Kafka (his real name) – the man had a *presence*. As he and his Troops left, the Sergeant directed us to not let anyone else in. Of course, we couldn't lock the doors with a show in progress and the building full of people, but we kept the entrance and foyer area clear. Well, except for one diminutive gentleman in a pork pie hat, South Seas shirt and Bermuda shorts.

There are three pairs of doors at each main entrance to the Coliseum. It became a frustrating comedy. This fellow would enter one door and Morgan would throw him out another. He'd come in a different door and Morgan repeated the process of evicting this guy, several times. I was no help at all, because I couldn't stop laughing. Finally Morgan guessed the correct re-entry door, met the culprit on his way in, blocked the entrance and sternly told the fellow, *"and stay out,"* while pulling the door shut with a resounding slam. By now we were thoroughly worn out. But we had done our job. We congratulated each other as the Mounties trotted into the arena – at last – to begin the Musical Ride of the Royal Canadian Mounted Police. **John Feeney**

Brittany Spears performing at the 2002 Fair. SF

Races

From the 1968 Fair official program book, a photo of harness racing, which was opened only to two-, three- and four-year old colts. NP

Note: Horse racing is a traditional and long-standing entertainment at fairs. The 1892 Fair featured horse racing. The NYS Racing Commission was established in 1896, but there was no horse racing at the Fair in 1899. However, in 1900, the State authorized $10,000 to create "the Syracuse Mile", a fast, one-mile race track at the Fair. Construction for the track began on May 1 that year and was completed by the August 1 deadline.

The first Hambletonian was raced in Syracuse in 1926. It was held there again in 1928. Harness racing continued until the early 1950s, resumed in 1964 (but presently is not conducted during Fair-time.) The New York State Harness Breeders' Association oversees the racing program and purse money; officials of the United States Trotting Association govern the program and sanction the races.

★ During Fair-week, auto race drivers would come to Syracuse. One race car driver, Deacon Litz, would fly his bi-plane into Amboy airport. Walter Stankwicz and I had an arrangement with the owners of the planes: we would clean the airplanes in exchange for a ride. That week we bicycled out to Amboy airport hoping that Deacon Litz would fly in. The owner of one plane owed us a ride and he asked Deacon Litz to "give the boys a ride." Litz was a stunt flyer as well as an auto racer and looped, dove and gave us the ride of our lives. *Joe Castellani*

★ The Syracuse 100 was a highlight of the New York State Fair. For a while in the early 1960s there was an effort made to convince the

State of New York to build a football stadium at the fairgrounds. The stadium would have replaced the track used at the time for a 100-mile Labor Day auto race, featuring cars and drivers that had raced at the Indianapolis 500 on Memorial Day. (Although they didn't do any actual filming there, the 1950 MGM film, *To Please a Lady*, had a race car driver played by Clark Gable going to Syracuse as part of his schedule.) The fairgrounds has a dirt track, and when there were 30-or-so racing cars zooming around, the dirt was flying everywhere. I watched two of those races from the top row of the Grandstand, as far from the track as a spectator could get, but the dirt started layering my face and chest almost immediately. Anyone you met on the way home knew without asking just where you had been. ***Jack Major***

★   Beginning when my nephews Patrick and AJ Lucas were about five and seven years old, they were involved in microd racing at the fairgrounds. This was a natural for them, given the family interest in cars and things motorized. At about the same time, their uncle Ric and I had begun to date and the family was growing inquisitive about the long-term nature of our relationship.

Microd racing consumes a large part of the spring through summer, with a break during the running of the Fair. By the Sunday of Memorial weekend, 1992, the boys were "seasoned" microders (ages eight and ten) and the season was in full tilt. Ric and I went to the track, knowing that the boys and their parents would be there. As we stood as a group, we engaged in general chatter, but I managed to arrange and re-arrange the caps that each of the boys wore, flashing a newly adorned left hand. My sister-in-law was first to notice the diamond engagement ring (I was trying hard enough). ***Judith LaManna Rivette***

★   Mom worked at the Fair when I was a child. After I was older she told me about Lucky Teeter, who raced at the Fair. We used to tell this joke all the time: "Who taught Lucky Teeter's wife to drive? Teeter taught her." ***Marley Olmstead Bruegger***

★   The auto races and shows at the New York State Fair were popular attractions in the 1930s and '40s. Demolition Derbies, long and short distance races drew regular crowds. But after World War II, the *big* race was on Labor Day and attracted huge crowds. In the days before the large parking lots were available, men (and the audience was

99% men) would park along Milton Ave in Solvay and its side streets. You always knew that it was a really big crowd when the cars lined Charles Ave (in east Solvay). From there the men walked a mile and a half just to get to the race track. ***Barbara S. Rivette***

Note: Auto racing was popular at the State Fair from its early years, until a major accident in 1911 - on the 44th lap of a 50-lap race – in which 11 persons were killed, many of them trackside spectators. There were no car races again until 1919. As of 1920, the one-mile dirt track at the Fair was recognized as one of the world's fastest tracks, over twenty racing records set there between 1920 and 1929.

From the 1940 Fair official program book, a photo advertising the Rocket Car Jump of Lucky Teeter, captioned: "Rated the most hazardous and difficult stunt ever conceived...Lucky Teeter sending a stock model sedan soaring clear over the full length of a huge transcontinental type bus. This perilous leap tops the list of twenty-eight events Lucky and his Hell Drivers will attempt four nights, starting Friday, August 13th, on the racetrack at the 100th Anniversary New York State Fair." NP

From the 1969 Fair official program book, advertising that year's stock car race, with $8,000 in prize money and $2,000 for the winner of the 30-mile feature race. From 70 to 90 cars were usually entered in this race that traditionally ran on Labor Day and used to run on the Saturday after Labor Day. NP

★   Before the war (World War II) the Fair ended on the Saturday after Labor Day and featured 100-mile race with cars from the Indianapolis Circuit. If you stood along the rail near a curve you would put a grocery bag over your head (with holes cut out for your eyes to protect yourself from dust and clumps of dirt. We had a different seating arrangement. We would go in the morning, bring a sandwich and sit on crates on the second floor of the Poultry Building, facing the track, giving us an unobstructed view of the first turn and back stretch. We played pitch and read the Post Standard until the race started. One drawback was that the Poultry Building is the noisiest building of the Fair. There were also harness and motorcycle races. There was this odor from the castor oil from the motorcycles that you could smell all the way to Solvay. *John Neary*

A post card showing motorcycle racing at the Fair grounds, probably in the very early 1900s. PC

Food and Give-Aways

★   The NY State Fair wouldn't be "The Fair", without having a delicious baked potato. Presently I am the Superintendent, Fruit and Farm Products, at the Fair, but I have been associated with the Potato Booth in the Horticulture Building in many capacities for about 30 years. (The license plate on my car is: MS POTATO). Over these years, I have witnessed about 1.2 million potatoes being consumed.

In the 1970s, the Empire State Potato Club, Inc. and the NYS Department of Agriculture and Markets joined forces to promote New

From the 1994 Fair, the NYS Potatoes and the Big Apple (Melissa Daino) at one of the daily afternoon parades. PHOTO BY MARY ELLEN DAINO

York State Potatoes. That's when the Potato Booth started. The many sponsors of the booth donated the potatoes and butter and all related items. The workers all donated their time. It started out as giving away a half of a baked potato free and in those early years many, many folks waited in long lines to receive one. As the years went by, the lines got longer. Some wait for at least an hour.

Beginning in 1992, we started selling a whole baked potato for $1, mostly to offset our increased expenses. There are still the same long lines of people waiting for a baked potato, even though every day you hear someone say, "I remember when they were free." Now, even with our additional ovens, we still can't keep up with the Potato Lovers' demand. We serve about 30,000 potatoes in twelve days, and they are still the best buy at the NY State Fair. **Reta Amidon**

★   It was at the State Fair that I drank my first soda. A friend and her niece came to the Fair with us. When we stopped for lunch, Shirley ordered a hot dog and root beer. I ordered the same. That was my first experience drinking a carbonated beverage. I didn't know I was supposed to open my mouth when I burped. I thought I'd ruined my nose forever. **Marion Tickner**

★   I visit the Fair daily, so to keep costs down some, I often scout out inexpensive foods – $1 for a great baked potato, 25¢ for icy cold milk or maybe 50¢ for a P&C soda. Then for dessert there are samples – you just have to know where to find them, like that maple cotton candy or fudge. For a snack later, some pretzels and dip.

On the other hand, I do treat myself to some special food items. One day of my visits to the Fair is set aside for a sausage sandwich (I have my favorite spot). Another day, the treat will be an apple dumpling smothered with ice cream, chocolate, strawberries, caramel and whipped cream. Only once a year, so those calories don't count. **Carol L. Cook**

★   As a child going to the Fair with my parents in the `60s, and with my saved-up money, I always made sure that I had enough money to buy a Walk-Away Sundae every year. That was my treat for the day. **Jill Ladd**

★   Food has also always been a huge part of my Fair experience. It is at the Fair where I tasted strawberry shortcake for the first time.

Every Fairgoer has their one food that a trip to the Fair would be incomplete without. My mother's favorite treat is fried dough (she always gets it right before she leaves, so it's a nice and gooey treat for the ride home). For my friends Cinzia and Amanda, it is a deep-fried onion and roasted corn, respectively. I can't live without an apple dumpling. No matter what area of the fairgrounds we happen to be at, when it comes that time, we will head completely out of our way in order to taste our special treat.

A few years back, a friend decided to take a fried-onion home with her in her backpack. It might have been a great idea, if we had gotten it right before we left for home and not almost immediately after we arrived. By the end of the day, her backpack was ruined and we had left our mark, *literally*, at every Fair attraction we had been to. **Heather Brady**

★   "I lost 9 pounds in 12 days on the State Fair diet." Yup. After 12-13 days of eating first-rate Fair food and Midway selections, 12 days of lackadaisical meandering about accompanied by repeated napping

From the 1940, 100-year anniversary Fair, a souvenir WOODEN NICKEL – front and back – was printed on light balsa wood; the information printed on the back explains its value. PC

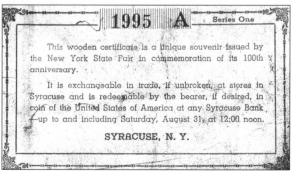

and vast quantities of munchies, I lost 9 pounds. Steak sandwiches, pizza, eggs sausage and potatoes, beer, wine and soda, fried chicken, fried chicken fingers, fried dough, French toast, and the plethora of goodies, all. I should market the concept. *Mark David Blum*

★   The stand with the maple syrup candy and the maple cotton candy is the best. It's a place I have to go to before I leave the Fair. And on a hot day, nothing is better than a large Hawaiian shaved ice. *Russell Cook*

★   One noontime at the Fair in about the late 1990s, my wife and I were sitting in our car having some lunch. It was very, very hot that day. We were parked near the Administration Building just outside of the Fair gates. A guy came over to us and asked us if we would like to try a new cereal. He was being paid to hand out the cereal box samples at the Fair. We agreed and he gave us four small boxes, two each. Only a short time later, the same guy asked us if we would like more cereal. He wanted to go home. He had us open the back door of our car and put in his whole supply. When we got home, we counted 78 cereal boxes. *Kenneth A. Williams*

★   The first thing my friends and I would do, after checking-in with Dad at the fairgrounds fire station when we got to the Fair, was to get in line for a free baked potato in the Horticultural Building. The Center of Progress was full of free samples of food, candy, fudge and treats and as we walked through the other buildings we collected a bag full of samples from vendors. A walk through the animal buildings; stop at the Coliseum to watch the horse judging; continue on to watch the Corn Dance in Indian Village and our last stop would be in the Dairy Building for a cup of milk and a taste of ice cream before walking home. *Judith Conway DeLucia*

★   My father, John Szczech, has told us of the very hard times during the Depression, when if Grandpa got a day and a half of work a week at Solvay Process, the family rejoiced. Some weeks Grandpa didn't even get a day of work there. All the boys were big eaters, and sometimes there just wasn't enough food. But during the Fair, the boys all got enough milk to drink.

From the time the farmers arrived at the Fair, a few days early, Dad and some of his brothers would get up a 4:30 a.m. and walk to the Fair with a bright, clean pail. They'd go to where the cows were getting their morning milking and give their pails to the farmers, who were generous about milking their cows into the pails. The boys would go from cow to cow until the pails were full. Then, with profuse thanks, the boys would carefully make their way back home with milk for the family. Later in the day, they went back to the Fair to soak-in the sights and sounds. They went *every* day. They snuck in through various loose fencing and the policemen looked the other way. Dad says that the memories of the State Fair are among the happiest of his childhood. *Elizabeth Szczech Segar*

★ In the 1930s and `40s, most people brought picnic lunches to the Fair. We always headed for the Dairy Building for iced cold strawberry, white or chocolate milk for only 5¢. ***Beverly Davis*** Note: In those days, in the 1930s and 40s, the strawberry flavored milk was considered pretty exotic.

★ Mom can sniff-out a baked bean sandwich anywhere, her *fav* sandwich of all time. She's been hooked since her discovery of this State Fair food offering as a young girl. When Mom was seven or eight years old, she attended the first post-war Fair. Some may recall the Fair did not operate during World War II. In those days, one went to the Fair all day, early morning 'til dark. For lunch, she and my grandparents discovered, for the very first time, the Grandma Brown's Baked Bean Sandwich doused with chili sauce, theirs for 5¢ at a small stand on the Fair grounds. Mmmm… As the day grew long, their stomachs growled for another baked bean sandwich. They returned to the stand only to find that Grandma Brown had sold out of her Fair fare. ***Catherine LaManna*** Note: Many people remember a baked-bean sandwich as part of their State Fair visit. Grandma Brown's baked bean company of Mexico would set up a stand at the Fair and sell the filling fare for a nickel or 10¢, memories differ. It was a hearty meal at any time of day. A slice of white bread, a layer of baked beans topped by another slice of bread. People stood in line for this simple meal during the 1930s and 1940s.

★ Fair going is a symphony of food smells. As my mother and I strolled through the perfume scents of flowers in the Horticulture Building, we were soon overcome by the smell of piping hot apple dumplings, served to us with vanilla ice cream and whipped cream topping. Passing the various vendors on the Midway, our attention could not be taken from the powerful scent of onions, peppers and sausage, which we consumed while lounging on a wooden bench, under a striped canopy. Looping around the Midway, we slurped blue raspberry snow-cones and then stopped to see the Clydesdale's graceful ballet. The scent of fried pizza dough soon tickled our noses and the sugar coated crispy foot long delight steamed as we tore it open. We sought refuge in a large fresh-squeezed lemonade and went to a show at the Grandstand. On our way out of the Fair, we passed a vendor cart that sold us a bag of cotton candy and a candy apple. To my mother Joanne and I, the Fair never smelled so good. *Brenda Lotito*

★ A give-away made it certain that I'd not soon forget my first State Fair date – no matter how much I wanted to. I was 14 and going with Joanne Maziuk, a Solvay High School classmate I'd met during our freshman year. We went to the Fair, visited all of the Fair buildings, strolled the Midway, ate a lot of Fair food, and, in general, did all of the Fair things that people do. It was a very pleasant day. Then we strolled through the building that houses chickens, ducks and other small farm animals.

I was a rather timid soul at the time, and had that look about me, I guess. So as Joanne and I headed for an exit, we were intercepted by a woman. Joanne stepped aside and made all the appropriate gestures behind the woman's back, but still my mouth couldn't find the words to get the woman to go away. Instead, I just handed the woman three dollars and scribbled my name and address on her clipboard.

It wasn't easy living that down, especially in front of my mother. Normally as sweet and forgiving as a person could be, every month Mom reminded me of the event. After the mailman came, she would say with a grin that was almost evil, "Here's what you've been waiting for," and she'd hand me the latest issue of Poultry Journal. My subscription eventually ran out, but I was kidded about that magazine for years. *Jack Major*

★ We always managed to find a free bag with handles to hold the literature we picked up, to be carried home, and usually trashed. The craziest thing that I did was to carry a yardstick home to my mother, which she used to crack me with when I did not mind her. *Mayola Willoughby*

★ My first job at the Fair was in 1938. I was 16 years old and I introduced "Blue Boy" tomato juice and gave out samples. The most fun job I ever had at the Fair was in the 1940s, when I worked for Pepsi-

Cola. I introduced Pepsi-Cola to Central New York by giving out samples in many different grocery store chains. I was "Miss Pepsi." Also at the Fair, we made records for people. Some people would sing, some would send a message, repeat vows, propose marriage, etc. That's when I found out so many people from other countries all over the world came to the Fair. **Madge Wells**

★ I have great memories of the State Fair. For all of us it was the end of summer and the beginning of a new school year. One memory I have is walking home over Bridge Street with my free, 5-pound bag of potatoes. We each got one so, between my seven siblings and myself I think Mom had enough potatoes to feed an army. Those days are gone, but will remain with me forever. **Mary Davis Doherty**

★ We get really good give-aways every year at the Fair. Like in 2001, we got some cool "I Love NY" buttons, TiVo pins and stuffed TiVo dudes, whole onions freshly yanked out of NYS soil, a Nurse Betty button and tongue depressor, a box of Jell-O, soda/beer can cozies, rubber jar grabbers, pencils, pens, plastic cups from the NYS Department of Corrections, spider rings, *The Conservationist* magazine, NYS bookmarks, recipes, a "Read My Lips, No New Texans" anti-George W. Bush for President button, a Jewish calendar *and* – the freebie of all freebies – a giant "2000" Jell-O mold straight from the Jell-O Museum in LeRoy, NY. **Laura and Ted Rozelsky**

★ One of the Fair's most popular eating places was the Solvay Tigers stand and the popular food there was "shells with sauce and meatballs." Members of the Tigers and its Auxiliary cooked and volunteered providing the food, counter service, and waitress duties through Fair-week. My aunts, Thelma and May Olgeaty, were among the volunteers. They enjoyed talking with everyone and soon the workers from the Midway became regulars at the stand, for the good food that was served. **Judith Conway DeLucia**

★ During Fair-week I held down a second job at the Fair as a waitress (college was expensive). I'd leave the Women's Building at 5 p.m. and walk over to work at Fort and Helen Cavallero's Italian food stand, which was behind the Horticulture Building against the racetrack fence. Cavallero's was unusual in that it had actual sit-down waitress service (the possibility of tips). By the time I stopped working at midnight, I felt pretty old. The worst time was when the auto races were running. Being right at the fence of the racetrack, the noise was deafening, and the stand would fill up with so much dust that we could taste it. **Susan Mascette Brandt**

★   Volunteering at the Solvay Tigers stand, was a time for all club members to do their part to raise funds for the CYC. Stand Managers Pat Pannetti and Frank LaPenna would organize work details to repair the wooden stand. It always seemed to have roof leaks, broken boards and a need for another coat of paint. Barney (Richard) Barnello would drive nails into every area, to hold the stand up. Dey (Daniel) Gallante and Saggy (Don) Salvetti painted everything that was not moving.

Before the Fair started, volunteers all signed in to a shift and were shuttled to the Fair. There, we were given a paper hat and apron and put to work. The jobs were very specific: you carried hot food from the kitchen to customers, you poured drinks, you wiped tables as customers left. The fun part of the job was calling out to friends and neighbors to come in and enjoy pasta and food being grilled by cooks Rudy Carducci and Bill Delfavero. When the work at the stand got a little slow, to pass the time we would shout to each other about how great we were at pouring draft beer with perfect "heads for drinking". John Simiele and Joe Franchini would identify their pouring skills by yelling out their Solvay High class year with each cup: "class of `62." **Vince Palerino**

★   Before Ronnie Phillips took over the concession at the New York State Fair Coliseum in the early 1950s, the State rented the building for $240/winter to store cars. It seemed that no one wanted to operate a stand or building where they wanted to have food sold. We brought the concession into the Coliseum in 1948. (Eventually we ended up with eight places.) We had to equip the restaurant and stands with everything to sell food, beer and a liquor bar. We even got tables and chairs, cash registers, grills, steam tables, etc.

We had great help in those days: Sam Mezzo and wife, Fannie; Tommy Greco and his family and Lucie, Mary and Rudy Tucci; Freddie and Billy (can't remember their last names) were our jolly two cooks; John Yoder was the Pay Master; Kay Luczyski, one of my great friends, helped a lot during those years, too.

A post card postmarked 1909, showing a "street scene" of the Fair. CONTRIBUTED BY DICK CASE

Being from the mid-west, I didn't know what Italian food was until I came to Syracuse, NY. My husband took me to a restaurant in Solvay, NY, where I met Annabelle Buzze. She taught me how to make meatballs and so many other things. The Buzze's helped at each Fair, too.

At the Coliseum we had the biggest beater that we used to stir our meatball mix in – ten pounds of hamburg at a time plus condiments, eggs, etc. We'd make the meatballs with ice cream scoops, put the balls on trays and bake them in the big ovens of the two huge stoves we had. We had a potato peeler and served real mashed potatoes. Our roast beef dinners, as I recall, were $1.25.

I used to put up cheesecloth on the windows in the kitchen, trying to keep the dirt from the cow showings from coming in one end of the Coliseum. In the evening, the horses came in the other end of the Coliseum.

It seemed to be the hottest place on earth during the Fair. We had more fans in more places, more flies, ran out of ice cubes and hoped it wouldn't rain the day and night before Labor Day, as we had a stand made out of metal Coke signs that Coke gave us. When it did rain and the car races started and finished for the day, it was so noisy when those balls of mud hit that food stand. To keep the kids off the roof was another big problem. ***Mona Phillips***

Food and Give-Aways • 55

Midway

★   Every year when I go to the State Fair I always ride a ride that I think is called the Tilt-a-Whirl. You spin really fast in circles. My sister is always afraid to go on it but to me it's really fun. I'm going on it ten times next year. *James Cerio*

★   The first time I went to the New York State Fair was in 1939. I was nine years old and had to ride around the grounds in a red wagon, pulled by my neighbor, because before going I had stepped on a board of nails and punctured my left foot. We went on all the "scary" rides and the last one was the "Loop-O-Plane." When we reached the top and it rolled over – out fell my bottle of chocolate milk and my nickels and

Tilt-a-World ride, undated. SF

dimes and pennies. Even at that tender age, I was embarrassed and never rode that ride again. **Thomas R. Demperio**

★ It's the little neighborhood that forms once a year for about twelve days or so between the popcorn stand on Montauk Ave and the stables on Belle Isle Ave: The Strates Shows, the midway, the carnival.

Just a small community of about 2,000 people. A train hauls the noise, the smells, the colors, the wonderful chaos onto the Fair grounds. Most of the Show rides to the Fair on flat railroad cars. Has about ten dormitory cars of two-man staterooms. You can see them lined up on the fairgrounds spur behind the Grandstand.

In addition to the regular year-round payroll of 250, the Show hires contract drivers and other help as needed, town to town. Needs the extra manpower to put up those rides. The Midway workers – who can't wait to get to a new fairgrounds and then can't wait to leave.

Ben Braunstein was considered family by the Strates Shows people. Signed-on with the Shows as a manager and public relations advisor. He'd call me a few weeks before the Strates crews started setting up in Lakeland each year and we'd meet. That call was like a trumpet blowing: the Fair was at the horizon. So was the end of summer.

By 1995 Jim, the only son of Strates Shows founder James E. Strates, took over the Show. Seems Daddy Strates wanted his boy to go to law school. Jim saw his future on the lot. Talked with one of his University teachers, who told him a year at the carnival was worth three in college. So it was "no" to law school, Jim told his father. His father replied by crossing himself and praying in Greek for God to help his son. Years later, his own children work for the Show as well, and not a single regret. Three generations of Strates. During the Fair, the Strates rule is to keep the grounds and Show "clean and cracking". No confrontations. They say a Strates Midway is a place of wholesome family entertainment, just keeping the people happy. **Dick Case**

★ In about 1938, the Strates Shows had a carnival inside big tents, behind the rides. There were freaks and fat ladies and girlie shows there. **Madge Wells**

★ My Aunt May Olgeaty was always lucky and she loved the Midway games. Sometimes the Midway workers – who she got to know when they ate at the Solvay Tigers stand – shared the secrets of winning the games of chance. When we brought our children to the Tigers' stand for supper, Aunt May would ask them what kind of stuffed animals they would like. Sure enough, she would appear after our meal with at least two stuffed animals for them to take home and treasure. *Judith Conway DeLucia*

★ When my mom and me went to the rides I didn't know which one to go on first. They all looked so wild that you just had to go on them. One of the rides that I went on was so, so wild that even my mom who wasn't even on it got dizzy and sick. After that ride I went on some more just like it. I just loved the wild rides. Best of all I loved the Fair. *Michelle Cooper*

★ In the early `30s when I was about eleven or twelve years old, I was watching a side show, when I was called to stand on the stage and had to stand next to the "Wild Man." He glared at me and I was so frightened that I bolted from the stage. *Arthur Tindall*

★ My favorite experience at the State Fair took place last year. I like the rides and went on all the big rides. (I'll go on any ride, except the Fireball.) The Ferris wheel looks so cool at nighttime. My favorite ride in the whole place is the Pirate Ship. The Midway is more fun at nighttime, and when you have money. *Kevin Revette II*

★ My mother and her twin sister – both newlyweds in the mid-1920s – went to a Fortune Teller at the Fair. The Fortune Teller told them to bring her new, hand-made, embroidered pillowcases, towels and tablecloths, in order to lift some form of "curse" that was on them. I guess they felt they had to give her what she wanted, believing that whatever "the curse" was would happen if they didn't comply. Apparently, when the Fortune Teller chatted with them before telling their fortune she had picked up on the fact that they made those sorts of embroidered items. Both new husbands went through the wall when they saw, later, how their wives had been duped. *Jane Campbell*

★ The best part of the Fair is the games. I could spend the day playing the water game or "I GOT IT". I've been lucky playing both. The last time I won a water game, I won a great big dog – bigger than me. I was really happy until I realized I had to carry it around the Fair until I went home. *Russell Cook*

★ Rides have always been a huge part of my Fair experience, especially during my teen years. One year, my friend Amanda and I met a girl in the Ghost Train line who said that the Double Ferris Wheel was the best ride at the Fair. We decided to try it. Big mistake. We didn't notice that no one else was in line. We didn't notice the open, rocking cars. In short order we began to feel as though we would be dumped out, each time we neared the top of the ride. It helped us a little when we tried to calm ourselves by singing Simon and Garfunkel songs. But by the fifth rotation or so, absolute terror had set in. No help that the operator thought that he was doing us a favor by giving us an extra long ride. By the end, we were laughing, crying, and never so relieved to be back on the ground. *Heather Brady*

★ The miniature train that was set up at the Fair was the same one that my cousin Don Neary operated in the summer at Suburban Park, Manlius. He worked at the Park as a conductor of the miniature railroad train. I spent many happy hours on that train, riding around the Fair. *John Neary*

★ The Ultimate Drop is a ride at the Fair where you are put in a metal cage and raised 100' in the air, then dropped 80 m.p.h. to the ground on your back, where they catch you in a sponge that is blue and yellow and full of air. They put a harness on me and I got into the cage, followed by two other people. We started to go higher and higher up in the air. I was sort of scared at first, but then I got used to being up that high. The instructor explained to us how to drop and fall and then it was my turn. I dropped. It felt like it lasted two seconds. Then I hit the sponge and the crowd cheered. I got out of the harness and went back to my terrified mother and brother who were waiting for me on the ground. That was probably one of the most exciting things I have ever done. *Fallon Rogers*

★ Last summer I went to the Fair with some of my friends and they all said they wanted to go ride the Top Spin. When I told them I had never gone on that ride, they looked surprised, like they had been on the ride many times. We got in line for the ride, waited a while and finally it was our turn to go on. The guy opened the gate and I went on and then I realized my friends had not followed. They were standing by the exit gate and laughing at me – they had chickened-out. Then the lap bar came down and even though I was real nervous, I didn't show it. The ride was a blast. Afterward, my fiends – that bunch of chickens – went on the ride for the first time. I can't wait 'til next year to see what will happen. **Brenin Matticio**

★   Ronnie the Midway worker, whose place was next door to mine one year at the Fair, made me laugh at his same stupid joke, which he repeated all eight days of the Fair. While he sat on one of my chairs in front of his booth, he'd yell at the crowd at the top of his lungs, "Hey!" And then he'd add in a soft voice, "We're open." Folks seemed to love it. He then followed up with a blast from his stadium horn. You know. One of those long red plastic horns you blow in and really annoy every-body around you? During the 2004 Fair, I learned how to use a stadium horn. **Mark David Blum**

★   I remember going to the Fair between 1966 and 1968 with my best friend Norine Nicit, my boyfriend Tony Caffrey and others. The best part was going on a ride called the Himalayan. The ride catered to teenagers. It had a D-J that played rock and roll songs of the day. He'd periodically bark over the microphone, "Do you want to go faster?" and we'd all scream back, "Yes!" And the ride would go faster. He'd ask again, "Do you want to go faster?" then he would reverse it and go even faster backwards. We'd sing along and scream and go on as many times as we could. Those were wonderful, carefree days to be a teenager at the Fair. (To my knowledge the Himalayan is still at the Fair every year. I have gone on it many times in the last 30 years). **Charmaine Caselle Caffrey**

★   I like and hate the Enterprize. I like it because it's real fast. I hate it because I get dizzy. The Enterprize is crazy. I learned never to eat before you go on some rides. Yuk. **Jared Ott.**

Visit the

NEW YORK
STATE FAIR'S

1940

GORGEOUS! GLAMOROUS! SPECTACULAR!

JOY ZONE

FASCINATING, MODERNIZED AMUSEMENTS

James E. Strates Shows, Inc.

Mile Long Pleasure Trail

RADICAL NEW CONCEPTIONS IN
MIDWAY PRESENTATIONS

PREDOMINATING WORLD'S FAIR FEATURES COMBINED
WITH THE OUTSTANDING ATTRACTIONS OF
THE OUTDOOR SHOW WORLD

30—DOUBLE LENGTH RAILROAD CARS—30

LOADED TO CAPACITY WITH SUPERTENTED
ATTRACTIONS AND MASSIVE NEW
RIDING DEVICES

Dazzling, Entrancing Lighting Effects

James E. Strates Shows, Inc.

1940 PRESENTATION
At the New York State Fair

From the 1940 Fair official program book, promoting the Strates Midway Show. NP

People

★ This tin type photo is exactly 100 years old this year. It is of my Great Grandmother and Great Grandfather, Jenny and Wilbur Snyder. They are with Jenny's brother Fred and his wife Lillian Fulmer. They all lived on Heman Street in East Syracuse. Wilbur and Fred retired from the New York Central Railroad.

Grandmother Jenny loved to go to the Fair. She went at least twice a year. She must have passed that love on to me, because 100 years later I now work at the Great New York State Fair as an Account Executive in the Sales Department. **Linda Ryan**

From the 1905 Fair, Fred Fulmer, Wilbur Snyder (back, l-r), Lillian Fulmer and Jenny Snyder (seated, l-r). CONTRIBUTED BY LINDA RYAN

★ My dad – Fred Patuna – was called *Mr. State Fair*. He was the Superintendent of the Main Gate and chief ticket taker for over 25 years. Dad always dressed up each day of the Fair: suit, tie, and hat, no matter what the weather. He'd be at the gate at least fifteen minutes before they opened each day of the Fair. Dad always commented how he didn't realize how many friends he had – with many people claiming to be his relative or good friend and then asking to see him, all the time trying to get in for free. Dad was Fire Marshal of the City of Syracuse for

Eliseo Rossi of Utica, New York was also regularly referred to as Mr. State Fair. He was known to be the first in line to enter the Fair annually, riding his bicycle in from Utica in the early morning hours. In 1983, for example, he arrived at the Main Gate at about 4:30 a.m., according to local newspaper reports. Eliseo Rossi bicycled to the Fair well into his 80s. PHOTO BY AL EDISON, FROM THE HENRY SCHRAMM BOOK ON THE STATE FAIR.

many years and he would take the days of the run of the State Fair as his vacation. **Karen Nesci**

★   I grew up on a chicken farm near Liverpool. Each year Mr. Warren, the "chicken doctor," spent a day at our house vaccinating chickens. Usually it was a hot summer day and I took it upon myself to carry a jug of cold water down to where they worked in the back lot. Naturally, when the State Fair time came around, we visited the Poultry Building. My brother and I looked forward to seeing Mr. Warren there, because he would give each of us a dime for ice cream. **Marion Tickner**

★   As a child I attended the NY State Fair with my parents and younger sister. But my most memorable visit to the Fair was in 1951. I lived in Jordan and had just celebrated my sixteenth birthday, August 26. My best friend from Chittenango wanted me to spend the last few days before school started at her house.   While there, I met her boyfriend's cousin and he invited me to go to the State Fair with them. Well, you can't imagine how I felt walking hand in hand with this tall, handsome young man. We took in everything. The animals, the rides, the games and, of course, the food: sausage sandwiches, cotton candy, candy apples and ice cream. It was the first of many, many State Fair dates with him because we were married two years later. **Gail Draper**

★   My faith in humanity was restored. My assignments to Fair duty include the usual general hubbub, but then there's one of the true

VIPs of the grounds: Madge Wells, guest relations ambassador for the Fair. As of 1999, Madge had worked the Fair for a mere 61 years – called the Fair her "second home." Guest relations indeed. The human touch. Then there's the person who probably came to know the campers of the Fair better than anyone. Mary Kay Root. Worked Gate 7 at the far end of the Fair, almost in Lakeland, in charge of the weekly and daily camper parking. It helped that she also has had her own "little compound" there. Her own camper location, where there have been nightly cookouts for family and friends and theme events, too. ***Dick Case***

★   The State Fair certainly has a special place in my heart. I've gone to the Fair since before I can remember and racing cars was always in the experience.

As a young child, I went with my Dad to watch the Indy cars at the race track. We would sit in our favorite spot: the middle of the pond in the infield at the west end of the track. Later, we got interested in racing microds near the Indian Village. The fairgrounds became my "turf". So as a young, 20-something year old, you can imagine my joy in entering the Demolition Derby on the big track. My first year running was 1973.

Twenty years later, I found myself entering my 18th Derby and hanging out with the love of my life. I told her I was growing tired of thinking up themes to decorate the car with, so that year, I told her, it was only going to be paint and numbers. Little did she know, I had come up with an idea over a year before that I thought would be cool.

So, some time after dark at the Demolition Derby on Labor Day 1993 – with her kids, my kids, her mother and a bunch of our friends in the stands (only three of them knew) – out rolled my car. Written on its side was the message "PLEASE MARRY ME BONNIE". The car didn't compete too well, but it sure was a "hit" with the crowd anyway. So with a diamond in my pocket, I ran into the stands to receive a resounding "YES!"

This, however, was not the end of the story. Two years later, I was once again entered in the Demo Derby. This was my 20th event. It was less than three weeks before our wedding day, set for September 30. I had a car given to me by a co-worker and everyone began to tell me I was crazy to enter a K-car – but before my qualifying heat was over, that little front wheel drive gem had the crowd in a frenzy.

The race actually had gotten down to "the K-car" and a big old Cadillac. The Caddy was able to get behind me and push. Having lost my brakes long earlier in the race, I could not avoid being smashed into the outside wall. After the second shot at me, my car folded like an accordion. I was pinned against the steering wheel and my right foot went through the floorboard. I was done.

So, as my fiancé watched from trackside, they cut me out of the car and hauled me off to the hospital. Luckily, I had nothing worse than a badly scraped shin. I did however leave behind a lot of new fans, and I thank them for that. The wedding was still on. **Greg Miller**

From the 1993 Fair, the Demolition Derby marriage proposal car of Greg Miller.
PHOTO BY CORKY SPRAGUE

★ I've known Jimmy Strates since he was in his twenties. He was by far the most handsome man I had ever seen – more handsome than Robert Taylor or Cary Grant in their day. One time during the Fair, Jim came to a spaghetti dinner at my Mom's house, and my sister Roberta and sister-in-law Marcia just sat across the table from Jim and stared at him. They couldn't eat, he was that gorgeous. His Dad, the original Strates, was a big, strapping man and a former wrestler. I remember him, also, as being very generous. **Madge Wells**

★ I grew up in Syracuse. About seven years ago, I moved to Florida where I met my "soul mate." We got married in August 2000.

Although we could have gone anywhere for our honeymoon, we decided to visit Syracuse. I wanted to show my new husband where I grew up. And I wanted to show him the State Fair – so, yes, we went to the State Fair on our honeymoon. We did go up to Niagara Falls for a day trip, also, but our main entertainment that wonderful trip was the State Fair, where I introduced my husband to "salt potatoes" and all the rest of the yummy food you get only at the Fair – food you wait all year to taste. We just moved back to Syracuse, so this August my husband and I will be heading back to the Fair for our fifth wedding anniversary. *Tracey Leigh Magner*

From the 1994 Fair, the Nestle Quick Bunny. Characters like these roam the Fair, entertaining young and old. In recent years, Fair Sales Manager Jim Goss dressed in a "big purple dinosaur" costume (not Barney). Recalling that the temperature inside the costume was "only about 180°", he performed to small groups, gave out flags and roamed the Fair to the amusement of many children. From his description, it is hard to know who enjoyed it more – the kids, the parents or him. PHOTO BY MARY ELLEN DAINO

★ I happened to love the color purple back when my husband and I ran the food operation at the Coliseum. Our hockey team uniforms were purple and gold. Zinzi Mascetti – then in charge of maintenance – painted the Syracuse Sports Concession trash cans purple (well, actually a lavender) just for me. One night, my daughter (Barbara Phillips Iannuzzi) and I stayed up all night long popping corn with two big popcorn poppers. There was a big event going on and we had run out of popcorn the night before. We didn't have time to box all of that popcorn, though, so we took our Zinzi lavender trash cans, put in two plastic bags and filled each one with popcorn. We boxed it later. *Mona Phillips*

A post card of Empire Court, postmarked 1921. PC

★ The name "Tuzzolino" and the New York State fairgrounds go hand-in-hand. Anyone and everyone knows at least one Tuzzolino who has worked at the fairgrounds – no doubt, because the Tuzzolino's have worked their entire lives there.

Mom, Angie Tuzzolino, started work at the Fair over 50 years ago, supervising a crew of women who cleaned all the buildings on the grounds. This was at a time when everything was done by hand. The floors were hosed and covered with powdered lye soap, scrubbed with brooms and hosed off again. They worked extremely hard. When they worked during Fair-week, their work- day started just as the Fair was shutting down for the public and everyone was leaving. Back then the Fair was only seven days long. In 1981, Mom was promoted to Maintenance Dispatcher, working under Billy Isgar and Harold Wheeler. She retired in 1996, but she still comes back to help out with dispatching during Fair-week. She just picks up right where she left off. Mom loves the Fair and would not miss working at the Fair for the world. Since the fairgrounds were such a part of my mom's life, it was only natural that it would become a part of my sister's and my life. I started working at the Fair in 1967 and sister, Patti Tuzzolino, started in 1970. We worked alongside my mother and she taught us the ins and outs of life as a worker at the Fair. Patti now has her own crew and is in charge of the Dairy Products Building. When Mom retired in 1996, I was promoted to fill her position. Nine years later I am still at the Fair, dispatching, sitting in the chair my mother sat in when she retired.
Kathy Tuzzolino

★   My uncle, Canandaigua lawyer John Shea would attend the State Fair as his annual vacation. He would close his office, take the train to Syracuse and spend the week at the Fair, staying with his brother, Syracuse School Principal James Shea (Shea Middle School is named for him) and riding the trolley or bus to the Fair grounds. There he would spend each day taking in the sights and meeting old friends. He was so well known for this annual State Fair trip that he was written about in the Syracuse newspapers. Having grown up in Fabius, John Shea knew people from across Central New York and in those days he was one of the people that others went to the Fair to run into. ***Charles F. Shea***

From the 2004 Fair, the Harambe Youth Tent Banner. SF

★   Susan and Jerry Rinaldi were truly "happy campers" one day in August 2001. That day they got married at the Fair. It seemed a natural. Actually, once they decided to get married, it was the only place they could agree on for the nuptials. They were married on the makeshift yard of campsites – where the couple first were introduced to each other by fellow campers Wendy and Paul Seabrook.

Susan found planning the event at the Fair wasn't that difficult. She picked up the food they'd ordered for the reception the morning of the wedding. The family's long-time pastor, the Rev. Thomas Cooper (retired from St. Luke's Church in Camillus) just paused when the helicopter flew above the wedding party. A vocalist testing the sound system at the Grandstand for that night's show made for interesting background music.

After the wedding, a reception of about 50 guests, bride and groom hit the bricks for the Midway, where Saturday nights are really lively.

Yes, they were in their "wedding clothes" and yes, people looked. The couple had a honeymoon. One day in Alex Bay and then back to the campsite with their camping friends. *Dick Case*

★ About 18 to 20 years ago, the Fair was visited by a delegation of scientists and other professional people from mainland China. They were touring the eastern United States as an Agricultural Delegation, particularly interested in our Dairy Industry and how to bring it back to China. There were about 40 people in the group, counting translators, all dressed in a similar Chinese style of clothing. I was assigned to them for the day, to show them around. We went through the Dairy Building and I had arranged for them to be given samples of the cheese and other dairy products on leaving the building. All were offered the cheese and of the 40 people, most politely refused the samples. Possibly two or three people tried the cheese. Concerned, I asked the translator if I had done something wrong and he reminded me that most of the people on that tour were not raised on cheese and just might have been a little wary of that strange new food. *Bill Fredericks*

★ Three generations of the Wheeler family have worked at the Fair over the course of the last 79 years. Harold D. Wheeler started at the Fair in 1936 in the Maintenance Department and was a roofer at the time of his death in 1965. I began my career at the Fair in 1958 as a laborer, moving up until I became Maintenance Supervisor and Superintendent of Grounds, the title I held till I retired in 1996. While I worked the Fair, I saw the grounds transform to year-round use, with pipes laid for sewers for new bathrooms. The third generation Wheeler, Harold Daniel (Harry), started at the Fair in July of 1993 and is now an excellent plumber on the staff. *Harold C. Wheeler*

★ The warmest story I can tell about our Fair days actually happened after my son, Noah, had been microd racing at the fairgrounds for about three years. We had just bought another car, which was #38. We were standing there talking about how we were going to repaint and renumber it. Was it going to be #6 (after Mark Martin) or #8 (after Dale Jarrett)? The grandfather of the kid who used to race that car walked up to us and wanted to know if we knew what the #38 on it meant. He went on to explain that when he was dating his wife, there was a song out entitled "Three words with Eight Letters – I Love You." Hence the

38. Well, I talked it over with my son – who was 10 years old at the time – and we decided to keep the number 38 for the remainder of his microd career. **Donald Ennis**

★   Almost every year at Fair time, in that my dental office over Solvay Bank was close to the Fair, I would usually get a walk-in patient with a toothache. Most of those were the traveling workers from the Midway. One year one of those Midway workers came in and asked me if I would pull as many teeth as I could for $32, as that was all he had. He had quite a bit of alcohol in him, so I didn't have to use much Novocain. I did take out all the bad ones, even though it may have exceeded his budget. **William Falcone**

From the 2004 Fair, Arriana Smith, daughter of Kehala Greene and granddaughter of Orville and Nina Greene, members of the Tuscarora Turtle Clan of the Tuscarora Nation, near Niagara Falls, NY. Arriana is about two years old in this photo and was in Native dress for Tuscarora Day.
CONTRIBUTED BY JIM GOSS

★   The best part of the New York State Fair is its inclusiveness of all people. It is one of the only places where you can find people of every nationality, race and ethnic background. The Fair transcends age and gender as well. It provides an opportunity for people to learn about other cultures through exhibits such as the Indian Village and African displays. While enjoying new experiences, visitors from every walk of life enjoy the Fair food staples such as fried dough, cotton candy and candy apples. **Jenna LaManna**

Special Visitors

★   The year I returned from being in the Service I took a job at the Fair guessing ages and weights of passers-by. (Believe it or not, my boss' name for that job was Al Capone.) That year, Governor Thomas Dewey attended the Fair and people were rushing to see him. While the Governor and his entourage were pushing through the crowds near me, one of them accidentally knocked over my booth. A few of his special aides stopped to help me put my stand back together. That was my one and only experience working at the Fair and it was great. ***Tom Triscari***

★   Bobby Kennedy came to the 1964 State Fair. During that Fair Week 1964, I waited until Mrs. V (my boss and a true Republican) went into a meeting so that I could step out of the Women's Building for a few

Senator Hillary Clinton greeting the crowds at the Fair. SF

minutes and go cheer Bobby Kennedy. He was at the Fair making a campaign stop in his run for the Senate against her friend, Ken Keating. (Mrs. V would *not* have approved, but I didn't get caught). ***Susan Mascette Brandt***

★   One thing I love to do at the Fair is watch the people, and believe me it's an all day parade of sights passing by the booth we run. Some make you laugh and some make you sad. Some you just cannot believe. This is the Greatest Show On Earth.

On any given day you could never guess who you might see – including some of the most interesting and famous people. The list, of course, includes the Governors of NY (Mario Cuomo and George Pataki), the Mayors of Syracuse (past and present) and in 1995 a young Jeff Gordon and his wife Brooke stopped and asked us for directions (which I gave him after I asked for his autograph). When Steven Baldwin stopped by and made a purchase, he asked me if I knew where the *Niack* Mohawk building was. I told him how to get to the *Niagara* Mohawk building. I've seen Dustin Hoffman and his family. Many candidates for political office come to the Fair. When one politician stopped by and I asked him "How's your Dad?" he told me "He's great. Thanks for asking." That was Andrew Cuomo.

By far the most famous visitor to come to the Fair that I can remember was in 1999 when President Bill Clinton came, along with his wife Hillary and daughter Chelsea. His fleet of Chevy Suburbans stopped right in front of my booth. Out he jumped and the crowd roared. ***Sue Tacey Ostuni***

★   When Peter Cappuccilli, Jr. took over as State Fair Director, he asked me if I would like to serve as the "State Fair Dentist." I accepted graciously and have since had the pleasure of working with quite a few celebrities associated with the Fair. A few years ago, I treated James E. Strates of the Strates Show. The next day he sent me about six stuffed animals in appreciation for what I did. About three or four years ago, I was able to take care

Reba McEntire performing at the State Fair. SF

of a wisdom tooth problem for one of the Back Street Boys. Also about that same time ago I took care of a problem for one of Reba McEntire's dancers. Ms. McEntire sent me an autographed picture of her and also a baseball hat with "Reba" on the front, to thank me. **William Falcone**

★ I remember when Governor Averell Harriman came to the Fair. He wasn't given a very warm welcome because the Republicans were in office at that time and he was a Democrat. He was very stern and proper man. He didn't say much, but just shook your hand and smiled. Postmaster General James Farley came the same day and he was a very friendly, likeable person. He remembered all of the names of the office force. Governor Nelson Rockefeller was also a friendly person, always smiling, but his handshake felt like a dead fish. **Madge Wells**

★ My most memorable experience as Superintendent of the Witter Museum was to attend its 75th anniversary celebration in 2003. The event, supported by Friends of the Daniel P. Witter Agricultural Society, offered a grand array of food and beverages from New York State and many "friends", museum workers, New York State dignitaries and members of the New York State Agricultural Society were present. A special guest, a most dignified lady – Miriam Witter Walton, the grand-daughter of Daniel Parrish Witter – was also there. She had attended the actual opening of the museum in 1928, at the age of 15. At that anniversary event, my retirement as Superintendent was announced. Having myself had over 25 years of Fair experiences, I was very proud to be greeted so fondly by all my family at the Fair. **Millie Bankert**

A post card of Governor Hughes and State Fair Commissioners visiting the Fair, undated. (Hughes served as governor from 1907 through October, 1910.) PC

Note: President McKinley was shot during a visit to Buffalo just days before his planned visit to the Fair. When President Theodore Roosevelt visited the Fair, he gave a speech of almost a full hour to a crowd of 15,000 people. On their visit to the Fair, President William Howard Taft and his Vice President, James Sherman, interrupted the annual race when they drove past the Grandstand. In 1928, Amelia Earhart made an appearance at the Fair.

Events

A post card, showing new recruits, called "farm boys", lining up for rations in 1917 at the fairgrounds. CONTRIBUTED BY DICK CASE

★ In 1916, soldiers arrived in Lakeland to prepare for World War I. The State Fair grounds became Camp Syracuse, a training ground for 17,000 soldiers who spread themselves across 600 acres, including the south half of Lakeland. The sleepy lakeside farm community along Van Vleck Road, later State Fair Boulevard, turned into a teeming Army camp almost overnight. ***Dick Case***

Note: Even though the training camp was present, the Fair was held as usual in 1917 and 1918. Following the close of the 1918 Fair, a massive and devastating outbreak of Spanish Influenza struck, killing many area residents. The 1919 Fair was referred to as the "return to peacetime" fair. There was no Fair held from 1942 through 1947, during World War II.

★   During the early War years – in 1943 (when I was 17 years old) – I worked at the State Fair when it was used as a U.S. Air Force depot. We worked with all U.S. Air Force supplies. Each building was a different unit. It all had to do with the War. I was a Foreman in Building #6 and had 17 people under me. That was quite a chore for a young man.

One night when our shift was about to end, a dike broke near State Fair Boulevard and all the soda ash from the Process lime beds headed toward the fairgrounds. This stuff, if it hit your skin, it could burn you badly. It flooded the whole fairgrounds and the homes on the State Fair Boulevard. We heard the screams from the homes. We got in boats to go across the road and rescued quite a few adults and children. That was a night to remember as a young man, about to go to the War myself. I will never forget that night at the New York State Fair. **Rocco J. Chiaferi**

Looking down then tree-lined State Fair Boulevard, with the fairgrounds in the back, right, the white covering the ground is lime from the lime bed break; persons in the foreground are not identified. COURTESY OF THE SOLVAY PUBLIC LIBRARY

★   In recent years, the fairgrounds have become the site of more than just August activities. Living nearby in Lakeland, it is almost a sport to guess what might be going on based on what or who is parked in the nearby areas. Are all of those big boxy white metal behemoths waiting for the recreational vehicle show? Nope – they are trailers filled with crafts or antiques waiting to be loaded into one of the buildings. Boats in blue plastic all lined up outside the Center of Progress building means the boat show can't be far off. And all those station wagons with cages in the back? Cat show or dog show? Probably. Horse shows mean trailers and trailers and trailers lining the fence near State Fair Boulevard. *Barbara Lucas*

★   A spring dog show has been held at the Center of Progress building at the Fairgrounds every year for many years. In 1987, when I attended that show, I had just gotten a Sheltie dog – named Tawny – and had her in her very first obedience class. My wild dog badly needed obedience training so I was fascinated with the obedience dogs at the show and how well they were trained. As I watched, I told myself, "I want to do that." With no idea how to go about entering the show, I asked people there, and was directed to the Show Secretary's table. Following their directions I got put onto their mailing list for a premium (entry) for next year's dog show. That next year, I had Tawny prepared well enough to compete. She not only qualified but she was good enough to come in fourth in her rather large Novice A class. Consequently, I was bitten by the dog show bug and I have not missed that spring show at the Fairgrounds in 18 years. *Nancy Frakes*

Nancy Frakes with her 4-year old Sheltie (Onnaka), participants in the 2005 Dog Show. A dog show is an annual spring event at the fairgrounds. JLR

★   In the early 1960s, a public ice skating rink was built in the State Fair Coliseum for use from Thanksgiving into the spring. The cavernous Coliseum was chilly, but certainly warmer than skating outdoors. In fact, we kids sometimes skated in shorts, to the tune of canned organ music, and amid a lot of high school socializing.

Helen and Zinzi Mascette ran the ice skate rental and skate sharpening business at the Coliseum ice rink. The skate shop was in a tiny room under the bleachers, with a sharply slanted ceiling and barely enough room to turn around. Skates were shelved or hanging everywhere. (My husband recalls it looking like a clock shop of skates.) Mom and Dad would both finish work, eat a quick supper, and get to the skate shop by 6 p.m. each evening, working there with a space heater and a pot of coffee until the rink closed at 10 or 11 o'clock. Skate sharpening has a great smell (hot ground steel, graphite, oil, leather), and it seems like a thousand times that I saw Dad holding a skate upside down near his eye, setting a dime on the blade, and peering down the blade to make sure that he had sharpened it to a fine balance (all this for 50¢ a pair).

I think there may have been an ice rink in the Coliseum in the early `30s as well, because I recall Dad saying that he worked as a "rink rat" there while he was in Solvay High School.

On Saturday mornings, the rink was reserved for pick-up hockey games. Zinzi and his old hockey teammates from Solvay (Bill Galante, Danny Gettino, Harmon Tarolli and Pepe Miguel) would play against high school boys. These "old" guys (then in their late 40s) had been playing hockey together since they were children and had also played professionally in the minor leagues. Although age and weight had slowed them down, they were amazingly graceful and quick-footed on the ice, and what they lacked in speed, they made up for in finesse. They would come off the ice panting, but with huge smiles on their faces. *Susan Mascette Brandt*

★   It is a picnic with a theme, when the Car Club Association puts on a car show on the fairgrounds in the summer. Several years back, my husband, one of his visiting friends and I went to one of those open-admission (no theme car, all cars welcome) events on a sparkling weekend date, probably in early summer. Coolers were stashed inside of old Firebirds, Lincolns, Cameros. Lunches were spread on the hood of Franklins, Eldo's and Corvettes. People sat by their cars, others strolled

One of the many car shows held at the fairgrounds, circa 2003. PHOTO BY BARBARA LUCAS

by. There was live entertainment (oldies, of course) from the Empire Court stage. It was a slow, inviting, swarm of like-minded people, strangers for only minutes, until after the first words were uttered, "What year is she?" or "I used to have one of those," or "A Corvair? My Dad had one of those and my girlfriend and I used to make-out in the back seat of it when we were teenagers." *Judith LaManna Rivette*

★   During World War II the State Fair Grounds was an Air Force storage depot. In 1943, I was going to Solvay High School and worked nights at the fairgrounds, where I drove a forklift. Between the Center of Progress Building and Bridge Street there were three or four railroad sidings where we unloaded railroad cars of Air Force materiel.

On Thanksgiving Eve that year, I worked from 3 to 11:30 p.m. After I went home, the dike on the Process lime waste bed broke. (The area is now the upper parking lot for the Fair.) When I heard the news about it the next morning on the radio, I grabbed my 8-millimeter movie camera and went to Bridge St by the Fair's main entrance and filmed the terrible mess. The waste came across State Fair Boulevard, over the railroad tracks and flooded the Coliseum and the Midway. It went under the race track and covered the infield, which then held 55 gallon drums of aviation gas. The cleanup took months, but I have it on movie film. Oh, and that was the end of my working there. *Dick Forger*

★   In the mid-`40s I worked on the Solvay Process waste beds across from the fairgrounds. I was 17 years old. It was our job to keep the lime waste flowing so it would eventually harden. Little did we know that it would someday become a parking lot for the New York State Fair. **Thomas R. Demperio**

★   I can't even imagine how different my life would be without the fairgrounds. I'm there at least a couple of times a month, all year long. Besides the Fair every year, I've been on pit crews during Super Dirt week, shown goats and horses with the children. I've always had my New York State Inspector's class and test at the fairgrounds. We've played hockey at the Coliseum and have bought most of our hockey supplies at McKie Sports, where my son presently works part time. However, the biggest impact the fairgrounds had on my life came at the Microd track. It was always my favorite place to be with my son, Noah, who raced microds for ten years. **Donald Ennis**

From the 2002 Fair, New York State Governor George Pataki standing at the 9/11 Memorial after its dedication ceremony. SF

★   The 9/11 Memorial debuted at the 2002 Fair – made from a twisted piece of charred metal from the World Trade Towers, with an eternal flame imbedded in the Memorial. It was touching, how silently the people stood there, mostly strangers with ostensibly nothing in common. Yet as they stood before the Memorial, you could see the tenderness in their eyes, in a respectful silence of a shared sorrow. **Laura and Ted Rozelsky**

★   First the flags appeared, May 1, 2005. Thousands of them: 4,100 American flags positioned in the mound of grass in front of the Main Gate of the fairgrounds. You saw them when you waited for the light to turn onto `690, over near Crucible. One for each soldier from New York killed in combat in the Vietnam War. Volunteers from the

Operating Engineers' Union, Local 545 took three hours to put those flags in place.

Two days later, the bikers. About 3,000 of them: seven miles of motorcycles, escorting the truck that carried the 240 foot replica Memorial Wall, a slightly smaller version of the one in place in DC.

They started to assemble the Wall the next day. More volunteers: from the local trade unions, from framework to set-up; landscaping from Syracuse Parks workers and others. It came in pieces. Heavy stone-like panels etched with names, the names and names, of all 58,000 service men and women killed in that war of my generation. They carried those name panels reverently, in near silence, each to its place. Silence. To get the job done right. Together. It was the war of those workers to remember, their memory – panel by panel – going up there, in front of the fairgrounds. Later the names were read aloud. All of the names. It took 50 hours, to read them all. More volunteers. After that, it was disassembled. Packed-up. Moved on to the next city. At the fairgrounds, over 60,000 people saw it. Remembered. **Judith LaManna Rivette**

The traveling Vietnam Memorial as it was being assembled at the entry to the fairgrounds, May 2005. JLR

Sports

★   From 1936 through the mid-`60s the fairgrounds was a Mecca for sports. The Coliseum was home to boxing, hockey and NBA basketball, including the Syracuse Nats. The horse stables housed over 300 horses and during the off-season when the racetracks were closed, some 50 families, including their children, lived in trailers on the grounds. New Indy car races were also introduced sometime during one of Harold Creal's service as Director (1950-54; 1959-66). Such greats as A. J. Foyt and Johnnie Parsons drove in unforgettable races. *Harold C. Wheeler*

★   The State Fair is where I race my quarter midget (microd). I don't race it when the Fair is on, because they have go-carts racing on the track we use. When the Fair is over, I start racing again. My favorite

Microd racing at the fairgrounds, in 2000. AJ Lucas is in the pace (lead) car and Patrick Lucas is in the car named Metalica. PHOTO BY BARBARA LUCAS

race is during Dirt Week because there are people who come from all different states to race at the fairgrounds. There are usually 13 cars per race in my class. I got started when I was four years old and I have been racing for eight years and I have won five track championships at the State Fair. Come out and see me race on Friday nights at 7 p.m. **Sean Mulholland**

★   In the 1960s, an exhibition professional hockey team called the "Syracuse Stars" played at the ice rink at the State Fair Coliseum. The team was made up of 15 or 20 young Canadians, who would leave their day jobs to come down from Ottawa and Belleville every weekend and play against other teams on Saturday night and Sunday afternoon. Fans of the Stars will remember such players as Claude Charron, Andy Despard, Weiner Brown and Whitie Goeghan. Referee for these games was Zinzi Mascette, who had refereed hockey professionally for years.

Since it was non-league play, there was occasionally some clowning around on the ice, and the crowd loved it. Once, Weiner Brown wound up sliding down the ice on his knees due to an opponent's move that Weiner thought was illegal, but Dad thought not. As he slowly sailed down half the length of the ice, Weiner kept shouting, "Did you see that, Zinzi? Did you see that, Zinzi?" while Dad followed him down the ice shouting, "Yes, I did! Yes, I did!" The people in the stands roared.

The Russians were serious about their hockey, we learned, when a Soviet Army team came to town to play the Syracuse Stars, sometime in the middle of the Cold War. I remember Dad studying his referee's rulebook for weeks before the game. Syracuse's weekend warriors were leading after the first period, to everyone's delight, but the Russians eventually took over and won. Later, Dad figured out that between periods, the Russians had put fresh substitutes in wearing the sweaty jerseys. Syracuse fans consoled themselves that the Stars would have won if the Russians had only played fair. **Susan Mascette Brandt**

★   I don't recall baseball being played at the fairgrounds, but the Syracuse Nationals played at the State Fair Coliseum for a while during their early years in the National Basketball Association. The Syracuse Nationals, or "Nats", joined the National Basketball Association in 1949, after the merger of the National Basketball League and the Basketball Association of America. The Onondaga County War Memorial hadn't yet been built, so the Nats played their home games at the Jefferson

Street Armory downtown and at the State Fair Coliseum, the preferred location because it held more people.

During the early days of the NBA, the Syracuse crowd must have been one of the league's rowdiest, partly due to the David vs. Goliath nature of any game that pitted the small city Nats against teams from New York, Boston, Chicago and Philadelphia. At the Coliseum, baskets and backboards were mounted on Trojan Horse-like contraptions that were wheeled into place at each end of the floor, and were disassembled whenever the Coliseum was needed for another kind of event. Fans sitting near the baskets were known to jostle the foundations while an opposing player was shooting a foul, creating a kind of "Midway effect" (You know, "Step right up and try to put the ball through the swaying hoop!")

My father and I were at the Coliseum to see the first Minneapolis-Syracuse game. The most despised opponent, George Mikan, played for the Minneapolis Lakers. He was the wide-bodied, bespectacled giant who led the league in scoring. Oddly, I don't remember who won, though I did come away with a feeling that Mikan was one helluva guy because of the way he handled the crowd, which booed him unmercifully. Mikan wore a good-natured smile through it all, apparently enjoying the role of villain. Eventually the Nats became the Philadelphia `76ers.

Other teams used the Coliseum. Solvay High School had at least one game at the State Fair Coliseum – the Bearcats played North Syracuse at the Fairgrounds during the 1948-49 season, when they had a long winning streak and were attracting more people than the old high school gym could handle. Syracuse University played there in 1947, after Archbold Gymnasium burned down and before the War Memorial was built.

The Coliseum was a cold, cavernous place for basketball, with dressing rooms that would not impress today's NBA players. But because of its location – on the fairgrounds, so close to Solvay that we could claim it as our own – the Coliseum was always a special place. *Jack Major*

★ In about the summer of 1959, I, along with Bob May, made an agreement with then State Fair Director Cap (Harold) Creal to put an ice rink into the Coliseum. We thought it was a deal for only costing us about $1,000 a month – we had to build and install the ice rink ourselves – but forgot about the heating bill. Oh, well. We were pretty much out of money by the time the rink was made and the ice installed, so we took on another partner – Ron Phillips – who ran the food and bar concessions at the Coliseum at the time.

Among our other projects, at one point we contacted the Towns of Geddes, Lysander and Camillus and told them, "We'll skate your kids for 10¢ a head". The town leadership could not believe we could afford to do this. We told them, "We'll do it on Monday and Tuesday nights for two hours. You give us two police officers to watch over things generally and put your kids on the turnstiles to check the passes – we'll trust them to do that right – and we'll skate 'em." They got a big kick out of us, laughing that we'd never make a go of it. But we did. We made money at the concessions and skate shop and we made the Towns' kids very happy. *David McLaughlin*

Work and Jobs

Poster from the 1997 Fair. JPL

★   My State Fair experience was a simple introduction to the wonderful experience of giving back to our community as a volunteer. When I was a very young girl, seven or eight years of age (the timeframe being around 1957), my grandmother – Bess McGinn – volunteered, working in the infirmary at the Fair. At that time, that was where the NYS Troopers brought the children who had gotten lost. I will never forget the gentle kindness those giant men in uniform demonstrated in bringing these frightened children to be cared for until their frantic parents picked them up. The volunteers gently calmed the children. The women who ran the infirmary (and us young girls in training) offered the children food and drinks. This involvement has left a lasting impression of the importance of giving back to the community and some wonderful memories of a NYS Fair long ago. ***Maureen Wrightsman***

★   The main day of the Fair Week was the most exciting day – the day of the 100-mile dirt track auto race. And it was an opportunity for two teenagers, me and my life-time buddy, John LaManna, to make some money. Taking advantage of the fact that everyone was at the track, we would "liberate" the long benches from the Fair's bandstand and haul them over to the race track where we would sell space on them for 50¢ each. The spectators would stand on them for a better view of the race. John and I would keep on bringing benches over to the race as long as there were patrons willing to pay. ***Joe Castellani***

★   My dad, Frank Willoughby, always worked his 12-hour shift with the Solvay Fire Department when they protected the fairgrounds. During Fair week in the `50s thru the `90s they brought their fire truck and volunteer firemen to a small wood frame building located behind the Horticultural Building. My girlfriends and I would walk to the Fair and check-in with Dad at the fire station before we went on to see the Fair. ***Judith Conway DeLucia***

★   In 1963, while working as a commercial artist in the Syracuse area, the Fair became an account of the advertising agency I worked for. We did promotions and ads of all types: radio, TV, etc., and I got to design a new front entrance theme. I did this for five years.

Beginning in 1965, the Fair name was changed to "the New York State Exposition" (or the Expo). A story ran in the Herald-American on August 29 that included a map of the grounds that I drew (and I did it without the aid of computers, I might add). To me, it was a fun project – and I got paid for it. The Expo name lasted only a few years and reverted back to the "good ole New York State Fair." I was at the Fair about four years ago and have to say that to me it doesn't seem much changed from when I first saw it in 1939. A real fun place, still. ***Thomas R. Demperio*** Note: That map appears at the front of this book, between the Preface and the Introduction.

The Galeville Grocery "lucky duck." Bernie Rivers had this cartoon that I drew printed on the T-shirts we wore as we sold Lotto tickets at the 2001 Fair. JLR

★ In the spring of 2001, when Bernie Rivers (owner of the Galeville Grocery), told me that he was going to be the official New York State Lottery Agent at the 2001 Fair, I volunteered to help him sell tickets. I thought it would be fun, different. But as my actual scheduled work date neared, the idea seemed less appealing. Committed but reluctant, I reported for duty on my shift – one day couldn't be so bad. Bernie, Cliff Lowe or Marty Campbell were there to oversee operations and a variety of other people worked all kinds of shifts to handle the sales.

This was an amazing experience. We had a constant stream of ticket-buyers, each of four rows at least seven to twenty-five people deep almost all the time. What fun. And since more was better, I worked about three or four more days. I never took a break to see the Fair.

Galeville Grocery is the 2005 Official Lottery Agent. Maybe he'll let me help again this time and maybe I'll see you there. ***Judith LaManna Rivette***

★ In my teens, I worked the Fair week every year, to buy clothes for school. I did that until I joined the military in 1958. When I returned home, I continued to go to the Fair every year. I spend one day working at the fire prevention booth each year. ***John E. McLaughlin***

★ Our Security Department uses golf carts to get around the fair-grounds during the run of the Fair. At the 2004 Fair, Jimmy Walker, the Fair's Dispatcher, announced to us to be on the lookout for golf cart #81, reported as stolen. Whenever we get a report like that, I always take a ride over behind the Empire Room, because we find a lot of golf carts over there. On my way over there, another fair worker rode toward me from about where I was going. We stopped and talked about the broadcast and looking for the missing cart. As we went our separate ways, the other worker riding on cart #81, I called Dispatch on my radio to cancel the alert. *Edward Klamm*

★ One day when we were at the State Fair, we were watching this guy setting up his stand and he asked me if I wanted a job. I said "yes" and he said, "It pays 25¢ an hour."

What I did for that pay was to sit on a stool. Pretty soon people started to walk by and he started his spiel, talking about this new soap he was selling that had lemon and lanolin in it. It was a special soap, just coming out. The next thing I knew he was wetting my hair, took the soap and started soaping my hair all full of suds. Wouldn't you know, as the next group of ladies walked by one of them said, "Lena, isn't that Bob up there?" Lena – that was my mother – marched up to me asking me what I was doing. Proudly I told her that I was working, getting paid for the man to wash my hair. She walked away, shaking her head. I sat on that stool until 10 o'clock that night. I also worked for him the next morning, assembling small boxes and filling them with bars of soap that he had in bulk, in this huge box.

In all, I earned something like $6.75 for those two days of work, which I thought was pretty good pay for what I did. *Robert Doran*

★ Beginning in the 1960s and until I finished college, I worked at the State Fair every summer. Most years I worked the summer as an office assistant to Helen Bull Vandervort, who was Director of the Women's Building. At that time, the "Women's Program" meant exhibits and demonstrations on cooking, sewing and "The Arts" (things, apparently, that only women could be interested in), as well as a senior citizens center and short-term day care. Mrs. Vandervort was a classy, well-educated and slightly eccentric woman who was on a first-name basis with Governor Rockefeller and Senator Keating. She came from Ithaca, and there was a very strong connection between the Women's Building programs and the Cornell Home Economics School. I typed letters, paid the grocery bills of the Food Demonstration Kitchen, helped the "ladies" who ran the various programs and was a general go-fer for Mrs. V, who called me "Susu Dear." The Women's Building was cool and quiet in June and July, and I came to know every inch of it. During Fair Week, the place was crowded and hectic, but I wore my official Women's Building Staff badge and thought myself pretty important. *Susan Mascette Brandt*

★ In 1927, when I was 14 years old, I started working at the 4-H Club at the Fair. At that time they ate in the Clubhouse, which was a large wooden building situated in the back of the grounds, across from Halcomb Steel (now Crucible). Sometimes a Scottish band stayed downstairs there, and we enjoyed listening to them play their bagpipes.

The first year I worked there was all boys and one other girl (Helen Strickland). The boys used to help us clean up and get ready for dinner, so we would have time to walk around the Fair with them. What fun.

My first day at work, I dropped a small sauce dish and of course it broke. Out of a bedroom rushed this short, fat man (looked like he had a girdle on), and started yelling at me. I started crying and two of the waiters from downstairs were there and bawled out the man for making me cry. It helped. The man was the manager of the clubhouse. His name was Louie Long. My Mom worked there, too. She had charge of hiring the waitresses for the 4-H Club. **Frances Wall O'Neil**

★ Although I am at the Fair to provide demonstrations at the Wittier Agriculture Museum on making things with old woodworking tools, my skills got put to a real Fair job, in response to an unusual request from the New York State Fair Veterinarian. It seems that part of his responsibilities is to check horses for illegal drug use. How does one accomplish this? You guessed it – a urine sample. How do you get a horse to cooperate in this endeavor? I'm not sure. I don't think you just give the horse a cup and ask it to step into the "Stud's or Mare's Room". I do wonder if pouring water slowly into a tin bucket would encourage the same response in equines that it does in humans. Gratefully, I was not being consulted on how to get the horse to participate. The Vet's problem concerned the handle on the testing container – too short. So with the drawknife and spoke shave, I made two

A Fair bear, created by sculptor Brian Ruth, who in the last several years has created wood sculpted images with a chain saw about four times daily at the Fair. JLR

nice long walnut handles fitted to the testing containers. I doubt if the horses were impressed, but the Doc was grateful. *Nick (William) Nichols*

★ As young Solvay male college students, we looked for work at the State Fair before leaving for school. If picked by Zinzi Mascette (in charge of maintenance there), you were then assigned to grass cutting or trash pick up. You would cut grass by day, but for more pay we got to ride a trash truck from 4 - 12 p.m., pulling bags and cans from the vendors' stands. This was made memorable, as the vendors would reward us with some of their products. *Vince Palerino*

★ For the past 16 years, I have been the piano tuner for the Fair, tending to those needs for most all of the entertainers. For 13 of the last 16 years, I tuned for Stan Colella and in the last three years for his son, Lenny. One of my times doing this work, I came to the rescue of Arthur Duncan, the famous tap dancer with the Lawrence Welk Show. It was my third time working with the Welk people, as I recall, but the request for help came to me via Stan Colella. It seems that the taps had fallen off of Mr. Duncan's shoes and, while he had another pair at his hotel room, he didn't have the time to retrieve them. Stan asked me if I had some glue, to put the taps back on. I did. However, the glue (Tight Bond – that I used for my tuning work) was water-soluble, so I warned Mr. Duncan to not step into any puddles. The show went on that night with all taps in place. *Kenneth A. Williams*

★ On a cold winter night, I was working the graveyard shift (11:00 p.m. to 7 a.m.) for the Security Department at the fairgrounds. As part of our daily routine, it was my responsibility to go throughout the grounds and check all boiler closets. This particular night I entered the completely dark Art and Home Center. Armed with a set of keys and a flashlight, I opened the door and headed down the stairs toward the basement to check the boiler. As I started down the stairs, I heard the elevator doors close and the elevator moving. When I reached the landing, I heard the elevator also stop and the doors open. Thinking this very odd, I warily walked over to the elevator and shined my flashlight into it. Thankfully, no one and nothing was there. I went into the basement and completed my check and started back up the stairway.

To my amazement, as I was walking I again heard the elevator doors close and begin its ascent to the first floor. At this point, I didn't wish to investigate but hastily exited the building.

I sat in the patrol truck, breathing heavily and staring at the front door of the building. To this day, I am very leery whenever I enter that building. *Joe Klodzen*

★ Fair week and the weeks leading up to it, were busy ones for my father (Zinzi Mascette) when he worked up to 20 hours a day. My mother supported this by bringing him basket lunches and clean shirts, sometimes more than once a day. These "basket lunches" were extravagant, including homemade *macaroni* and meatballs, a nice salad, cloth *mopines* (napkins), and a couple of cold beers. Sometimes we would go along, having dinner for a family of four on some grassy spot off away from the crowds. *Alice M. Mascette*

★ My cousin Tom Smolinski and I spent the summer of 1955 working at the New York State Fair grounds as all-purpose housecleaners, dusting, sweeping, raking, shoveling – whatever it took to spruce up the buildings and grounds for the annual Fair, which that year, I believe, began on the last weekend in August.

It wasn't a fun job, but it did have its moments, sort of like present day reality television. We erected and worked on a scaffold at one of the buildings near Empire Court. I don't recall exactly what we did, only that I climbed metal bars in shoes that must have had leather soles. Nothing bad happened, but all the time I was climbing around I felt like the scaffold was made of ice. At ground level, our work was not physically exhausting, just mind-numbingly dull. Like the two days we very slowly walked around the mile-long dirt track that was used for the Labor Day 100-mile race that featured Indianapolis 500-style autos. Our job was to pick up stones, anything bigger than a BB. We had to make the track as smooth as possible. Later, Tom and I were assigned to clean out stables.

For us, our job got much more interesting once the Fair got underway. One highlight was getting the Coliseum ready for a Johnny Cash concert. Cash wasn't the larger-than-life figure he eventually would become; rather he was more rock 'n' roll than country, with a bad-boy edge that reminded me of Elvis. Tom and I were part of the crew that installed seats on the floor of the Coliseum and our reward was admission to the concert with the ability to wander at will. We, of course, wandered close to the stage and thoroughly enjoyed Cash's performance.

Afterward we went back to work, removing the chairs from the Coliseum floor. We hung around for a while and watched another crew lay down a basketball floor, though I don't know who played. The Syracuse Nationals were still around at that time, but it seems unlikely that they'd be playing a pre-season game before Labor Day, at least not back in 1955. *Jack Major*

★   We have several booths around the fairgrounds where we sell gum, cigarettes, etc. But people are always coming up to us and asking all kinds of questions – so we jokingly refer to our concession at the Fair as the "Other Information Booths". Honestly, at least half of the people who come up to our booths ask us questions or directions, such as: "Where's the Lotto booth?" or "Where can I buy film?" or "What about batteries?" "Where's the nearest ATM?" "Where's the horse barn?" "Where's the Grandstand?" and, the usual most frequently asked question, "Where is the closest bathroom?" I think the most asked question ever, though, was the year the Krispy Krème Donuts came to town. I finally put up a sign with an arrow on it to answer that one. *Sue Tacey Ostuni*

★   Before my children were old enough to go to the State Fair, I would get a baby-sitter for the day and go there to take pictures of exhibitors and their prizes. I collected the exhibitors' program of the Fair a week in advance, so I could locate people from the circulation areas of papers I knew would buy the photographs. Sometimes the exhibitors were old friends.

Having spent my four college years covering the Orange County Fair at the end of every summer for the Middletown Times-Herald, I had some experience photographing cows, horses, chickens, sheep, flowers and crops

A beaded leather pillow/pin cushion dated 1938, from Indian Village. NP

with their proud owners. Those Orange County 4-H'ers and growers taught me every trick of making any exhibit look good for the camera.

It takes a lot of positioning and timing to get each picture just right – so the flower's petals catch the light, or so an animal stands showing its best assets. And always so the exhibitor looks good. Cows need special work to get each leg correctly spotted – not too high, not too low on the uneven grass that looked so perfect in black and white. I met some very interesting people along the way while chasing down exhibitors or waiting for animals to be groomed to perfection. In the days before one-hour developing, Polaroid or digital cameras, there was a lot of stress waiting four days to see whether I had caught the rooster at the peak of perfection, with his proud owner smiling and prize ribbon draped just right. *Barbara S. Rivette*

★ When I was Ticket Manager, Governor Nelson Rockefeller's helicopter landed in front of my office one day. My windows were open and my tickets were in order in several open boxes. The helicopter rotors were spinning like no ending and my tickets flew all over the room – thousands of them, all over. I sat on the floor and cried. *Madge Wells*

From the 1969 Fair official program book (a theme of things futuristic), of "Miss Electra". NP

★ As a kid growing up in Lakeland, I rode the bus by the Fair every day to school in Solvay. Little did I think I'd end up in charge of the physical plant operations at the Fair as an adult. My first job at the New York State Fair was when I was 14 years old. I worked over by Restaurant Row where there was an agriculture exhibit showing New York technology on raising chickens and egg production. My job was to clean the chicken conveyor belts and cages. I tell folks I started my career right at the bowels of the Fair. *Bill Fredericks*

★ In 1972, my first night as Superintendent at the Witter Museum and the adjacent Van Wagenen Carriage Museum almost "went up in smoke." I had closed the museum and was making rounds. In the Carriage Museum there was an acrid smell and a screen of smoke. Was it possible that the building was burning? The blacksmith shop forge had been used that day and, sure enough, there was an "extended" fire in the forge area. After a call to Security, fire engines arrived and extinguished the fire, but the forge had been destroyed. Fortunately the blacksmith, Rob Shapiro, offered to rebuild the forge, and this time "with a fire box." His efforts proved to be a wonderful demonstration and learning experience for Fair visitors. The historic blacksmith shop was not damaged and to this day demonstrations at the forge delight Fairgoers. **Millie Bankert**

★ I have worked at the New York State Fair for over twenty-four years. In that time, I have seen many changes and have many memories. One of my favorite jobs during Tom Young's tenure as Director was in the Concessions Office, under Roger Mara. In that job I liked going out on the fairgrounds with my trusty orange spray paint, to mark the concession locations. **Mary Ellen Daino**

★ Back in the `60s during the Fair there was a pet shop in the southeast corner of the Center of Progress Building. One night the monkey cage wasn't shut tight and all six of the monkeys got out into the "structures" of the building, having a good old time, running over the beams and lights and decoration banners. Our Supervisor and the Building Manager had seven of us trying to catch the monkeys, climbing ladders and scaffolding and using fishnets. When we got to a place where the monkeys were, they would run some place else. We put on quite a show for the Fair-goers that day. I don't know who got the most laughs, the monkeys or us. And, after a whole day of wasted time, that night all the monkeys came back to their cage for food and water. When they got inside their cage, the door was shut catching all of them. **Harold C. Wheeler**

★ Mom had the job of assisting in staff hiring for the Boys' and Girls' Building in the 4-H Cafeteria and feeding the State Troopers. The many years she spent as Dietician (or cook) at Solvay High School and the fact that we lived on Hazard Street, helped a lot, since she knew so many of the local women and the hard working reliable young men in the vicinity. It was also natural that as each one of her children, relatives and friends reached the age to work there, we were hired – usually at 16 years old and before working papers were required. At the same time, Mrs. Valerio, of Cogswell Ave (Solvay) was in charge of the maintenance of the Boys' and Girls' Building. She hired workers from Solvay, too. Since cars were scarce in those days, everyone had to walk from Solvay to the Fair. My Dad would work (on vacation from Solvay Process) during Fair time with friends and relatives who were volunteer firemen from the Mountaintop, Prospect and Milton Ave fire Departments of Solvay. The boys did all the hard labor in the scullery and bringing up the heavy vegetables. The girls mostly worked helping to prepare and serve the meals and worked around the tables in the cafeteria. We got to know many new people, both young and old. We toured the Fair on our time off (as long as we were on time for the meals). In later years, most of us would take our vacation time from our regular jobs, in order to work at the Fair. **Robert E. Wall**

A post card of Empire Court, taken some time after 1912, the year the Dairy Building (background) was built. PC

Weather

❖•❧

★ August 1948. It poured rain for three days and I thought the Fair would be closed. I guessed wrong. It was 3:00 p.m. on the third rainy day and there I was, standing in the rain and watching a man and woman about 100 feet in the air. They were doing acrobatic stunts while the iron pole they were atop was swaying in the wind. It made me dizzy to watch, my head cranked back as far as it could bend and the rain hitting my face like BBs. I marveled at the skill of the two performers. Two days later, I wound up with a bad case of the flu and missed a week of school and football practice. It was worth it.
Thomas R. Demperio

From the 1995 Fair, the Coronas Circus, free entertainment. SF

★ One year I agreed to go to the Fair with my wife Jean on an evening when Helen Reddy was performing in Empire Court. Our plan was to also have our annual event, our State Fair dinner: sausage sandwich and beer. That day, it rained and poured non-stop. When I got home from work I suggested to Jean that she wouldn't want to go to the Fair that night, if it continued to pour. "Well" she said, "this from you, who golfs in the rain? And fishes in the rain? Pack your expensive rain gear. We're going". We did go, and it was great. The Empire court was packed to see Helen Reddy in the pouring rain. **Bernard Rivers**

★   I can remember getting flooded out at the Fair with water running right down the street about shin high. **Shamone Burton**

★   On a Fair-going day in 1949, I learned to not overdress when going to the Fair – less is best. It was when the Fair opened after World War II. On one very hot and humid week – it was easily over 80° – my friend and her boyfriend, my boyfriend (now my husband) and I went to the Fair. It was an era when people dressed up, and we went totally dressed up (including girdles, nylons and the boys had on suits, ties and the whole bit). There was some kind of car race on the racetrack and the dirt and dust was flying. All of the refreshment stands ran out of ice, as the traffic was so backed up that the ice trucks couldn't get through. **Jean Avery**

Poster from the 1903 Fair. JPL

★ Late on a Sunday afternoon, the skies opened up again and the rain really came down, for more than an hour. While we had the great flood, and there was a relatively steady breeze, my friend Ronnie (who operates the booth next to ours and sells stuff) brought out a plastic, air-filled dolphin. He placed it in the water and let the wind carry it down the street. Soon, everybody standing around was involved and encouraging the dolphin to swim. Blow-up dolphin races – something to do in the rain. That is, until the drains are cleared. In the slowly falling rain, people begin to move on. **Mark David Blum**

★ One year, during one of the Fair's infamous rainstorms, I hid for shelter under a "Jones, I GOT IT" tent. We were also trying to protect my friend Amanda's newly won hermit crab from getting drenched. **Heather Brady**

★ We got to hang out in the buildings after hours at the Fair in 2001. They kept them open past closing time that year because of a massive downpour. **Laura and Ted Rozelsky**

❧❦

The Labor Day Storm

❧❦

★ The year was 1998. Having been judged a section winner in the Culinary Arts and Crafts Division of the Fair, I was told to rebake my entry for Grand Competition judging to be held on Labor Day. I started to bake the night before. The storm that was brewing outside became worse, with wind and rain. My electricity went out (which effected my oven), so I took my ingredients across the street to my daughter's home. She had a gas oven. I baked by candlelight. The next morning we awoke to the news that the storm had been a tornado that hit Syracuse and that the Fair was cancelled for Labor Day. The fairgrounds were in bad shape. Greatly disappointed, but understanding, my family enjoyed my entry for lunch that day. (After the storm, the Competition Judges met, reviewed the entries, and chose me Culinary Grand Champion and Best of Fair for my Chicken Salad in a Basket.) **Agnes Adams**

★ The weather during the Fair at best is unpredictable and at times quite remarkable. Flooding occurred during the years I worked in the wool center, often times isolating Fair visitors in the building because the roadway on either side was river-like.

For many years I spent the run of the Fair staying at the fairgrounds. The wool center opposite the sheep barn was my "home" during the Fair from 1981-1991. One night during a dreadful downpour I was awakened and surprised, when I got out of bed, to step into several inches of water that was running through the building.

During the Fair of 1998, I stayed in a camper on the infield at the fairgrounds. Sleeping in a camper was a new experience for me. So, when around 1:30 a.m., I awoke being shaken about by a force unknown – no lights anywhere – my imagination went into high gear. I could hear the roar of the wind and a heavy downpour of rain with what I thought was thunder. I dared to look out, seeing several tarps blown askew and campers turned on-end. People were scurrying about and I realized an evacuation was in good order. A neighbor camper rode with me to the upper parking lot as per direction, where we stayed until after dawn. It was to be the last day of the Fair – on Labor Day. But sadly, the devastation had closed the Fair early. **Millie Bankert**

★ In Florida on Labor Day a few years ago, we heard a radio report of a big windstorm with injuries and damages to property at the NY State Fair and downtown Syracuse, NY. It made it seem like the Fair and Syracuse were the same place, but old timers like us from Solvay know that the Fair was in our back yard, in the Town of Geddes. **Mayola Willoughby**

★ It has become known as the Labor Day Storm, it was a Monday in September 1998, around 1:15 am. It was just a few hours before what I was hoping would be a great Labor Day. That's the day I always look forward to – it is bittersweet. On one hand I'm sorry to see the Fair end, on the other side I'm ready to get back to Tennessee. I usually go around and say my good-byes to all the vendors and friends: the people in Administration and the Maintenance people (who are always there for me). Usually, it's a lot of hugs and crying, but we all say, "See you next year".

That Sunday night was especially warm. The moon was full and beautiful; it lit up the sky. I went over to Cole Court to see Frank

Sinatra, Jr. sing. He was awesome, and everyone was in a festive mood. We closed up the booths and went home. One particular thing happened that night: three of my workers told me they were going to go back to the Fair for a party, but I told them, "You know it's late and I really need you guys to be with me tomorrow." Well, I guess they decided to go home and sleep and I'm so thankful they did. When the storm hit, two people were killed – it was awful. It looked like a war zone and the Fair was canceled for the first time since WW II. I think it was a blessing most of the people were gone by then, otherwise, the injuries could have been enormous. When I got there I couldn't believe my eyes. It was total destruction. I guess we'll all remember that year. *Sue Tacy Ostuni*

From the 1998 Fair, showing the Labor Day Storm damage to the Dinosaur Bar-B-Que food stand on Empire/Cole Court. PHOTO BY SUSAN TACY OSTUNI

Fair Life

★   There are some people who come and camp at the Fair as a family tradition. I know families that go back three generations – all coming to the Fair and staying the week. For some it's an annual reunion, seeing old friends and recreating their neighborhood. For some it is the annual vacation. One man told me he comes to the Fair every year, for all twelve days and brings $100 for each day. He spends his time playing the games on the Midway, pacing it so that the money is gone about the same time as the Fair ends. **Bill Fredericks**

★   The infield of the Fair racetrack has had plenty going on over the years. Some time ago, it was a lagoon. Even water-skiing demonstrations on the pond. It's also been used for several types of parking. No one lives at the fair year-around like they used to. Until maybe the early 1980s, when officials shut it down, the fair had a little settlement of 20 to 30 mobile homes in the northeast corner, next to the stables. The place was home to trainers, drivers and owners of horses.

More recently, the last 20 years or so, the infield's been used for camping. Fair's not in the campground business. Makes parking and some power and water hookups available, though. Spaces get filled on a "first come-first served basis". The Sunday before the start of a Fair regularly finds campers lined up at the gate – beginning even a week before – to get their desired lot. Favorites depends on tradition, distance preference – nearer or farther away – and friendship neighborhoods going back for years. Includes kids, grandkids, dogs, fences, signs, picnic tables, flags, coolers, clotheslines, TVs, even bicycles.

Campers can leave the Fair any time – usually they do to go for groceries. Spend time sitting around during the heat of the day. Go out when the crowds start to thin out. Paul Seabrook has camped at the Fair with his wife Wendy for many, many years. Their real home is only miles away, in Lakeland. Some years he's thought to not do it again. Then, what Wendy calls "the tradition" kicks in. As Paul Seabrook explained, "Its just neighbors and friends, year after year. ... I won't ever give it up." **Dick Case**

★ We camp at the State Fair. We don't live too far from the Fair, but it's nice to have a location for the kids to gather and rest and have a snack while being at the Fair all day and night. Last year was quite tough in a tent, because it rained a lot. We bring kids with us besides our own and their parents come for the day, too, to see the Fair and enjoy. There is so much to do: music all day, various exhibits and shows. We have met so many nice people every year that camp too. **Kathy Lawler**

From the 1969 Fair official program book (a theme of things futuristic), of the Rocket Belt demonstrtion. NP

★ Just before the 2004 Fair, the fair-grounds received some office furniture surplused from Agriculture and Markets, which replaced some older and rental pieces. During the summer Josh Reep of the Concessions Office picked-out a big, very nice desk that had a cherry-wood looking finish. It was all set up in his office and working fine for him. But on the first day of the 2004 Fair, when Josh went to his office, what he found was a large hunk of wood on top of some milk crates. Mystery solved, they had taken out the desk to set up for Governor Pataki to sit at to sign some bill into law on opening day. **Nick Pirro, Jr.**

★ Beginning when I was about ten years old or so, I would always spend one day of Fair-week shadowing my father. (This predates "Bring your Daughter to Work Day" by about 30 years.) I would ride the truck, answer his radio for him, help rake out storm drains, make his stops with him and visit with the Troopers at their headquarters.

My favorite Fair-week tradition was Dinner on the Dump. Getting ready for this meal, we would arm ourselves with a couple of rolls of paper towels (to use as a tablecloth) and stop at the Horticulture Building, where the guy in charge of the fruit and vegetable competition would give us yesterday's First Prize tomatoes, cantaloupes, whatever. We'd then take our plunder out to the dump, which is also where Bob Baker's Barbecue roasted their hundreds of chickens to stock their popular stand on the crowded Midway. A couple of their chickens added to the meal. Dad's curved roofing knife, quickly polished with the paper towels, was used to slice the cantaloupe. I would "set the truck" by putting paper towels along the back edge of the truck bed, and we would stand in the dump enjoying our delicious fresh dinner off the back of the truck. *Alice M. Mascette*

★ When Joe O'Hara was Fair Director, I was his secretary. It was a delight when Joe's children, nieces and nephews spent the night during the Fair in Joe's office. You would see them all lined up on the floor at night and waking up in the morning excited and ready for a fun-filled day. We would also have a Fair Family Picnic that included all staff members and their families. We had a great time – games for the children, water tube races in the pool in front of the Horticulture Building, karaoke and lots of other fun things. Today, I am the Entry Department Coordinator. Under Peter Cappuccilli as Fair Director, we play Fair Trivia at our many employee gatherings. *Mary Ellen Daino*

★   At the 4-H Building, it was still dark when breakfast was served. The 4-H-ers had to be up early to feed and milk their animals by hand, so we had to be up before them to get the meal. Nevertheless, working there proved to be a worthwhile job. One day, we discovered that the mischievous 4-H boys (who stayed in the upstairs dormitory) had filled the sugar bowls with salt and the salt shakers with sugar. Upon discovering the practical joke, the girls had to refill the containers with the correct condiments, but the mixed sugar and salt was not wasted. It went to the chef to be used in the cooking. **Robert E. Wall**

★   I just realized something. It is a non-stop party and reunion when I see my "Fair friends." We see each other only once a year and during the two weeks we are together, we become a sort of clan. The last day of the Fair, you hope for one last chance to say goodbye. That's the time that everybody is so busy. One minute they are rushing to pack ... and the next minute they are gone and so are you. The lights and sounds of the midway at night are overwhelming. On a weekend night, they overpower you. When it is a weekend night and the last night of the Fair, the electricity hits you like a bolt of lightening. **Mark David Blum**

★   The Fair was very, very much a part of our family's life. I remember going to the Fair *every day* of Fair-week until I was in my 20s; eating Mexican Walk-Away Sundaes on the Midway; always going to my favorite place, the Indian Village; riding with my Dad in his State Fair Maintenance stake truck, and shouting together every time we drove down the underpass under the racetrack; learning to drive on the fairgrounds in deep snow in February 1963; and, more times than I can count, having someone connected somehow with the Fair say to me, "Ain't you Zinzi's kid?" **Susan Mascette Brandt**

Robert Maxwell at his Walk-Away Sundae stand at the Fair.
CONTRIBUTED BY BETTE MAXWELL

★   As manager of the Art and Home Center, I attend a staff meeting each morning before the Fair opens. One morning we were discussing that there seemed to be many dogs that year on the Fair grounds. We were advised – if we saw any – to tell the Fair-goer that generally dogs are not permitted on the grounds. As it happened that afternoon I saw a woman walking through my building with a very small dog in her arms. Being a dog lover myself, I approached the woman to explain that as much as I loved dogs, they were not allowed on the Fair grounds. The woman quickly replied, "Oh, she hasn't been on the ground. I've been holding her all day." **Mary Lou Sobon**

★   As we Burton kids got older and could drive ourselves, we started going to the Fair and staying for the weekends. We would bring tents and even sleep in the trunk of our car with it opened. We loved the Fair so much.

Now that we are older and have families of our own, we all (my mother too) take campers and camp for two weeks plus. We actually go to the fairgrounds ahead of time (for the pre-Fair) so we can get a spot and all camp together, a lot of us taking our vacations from work to go. We bring a kiddie pool w/slide, cookers, freezers, big party tents, we make a vacation out of it. Last year we got six spots together and formed a big square, with a space in the middle almost the size of a football field. Our kids have worked the Fair, so have my sisters. We all just have a great time. **Shamone Burton**

★   Everyone who works at the Fair has his or her own little neighborhood and network. Without these people around you it would be lonely. We look out for each other, anything I need, all I have to do is ask and five people are there. My block of Fair neighbors are some of the finest people you'd want to know. We are of all different ethnic backgrounds, religions, ages, and from different parts of the US, but for twelve days we all bond. If I had to say one thing that describes my New York State Fair experience it would be that no matter where you come from or where you are headed, for twelve days you are a member of the Fair. **Sue Tacy Ostuni**

The Experience

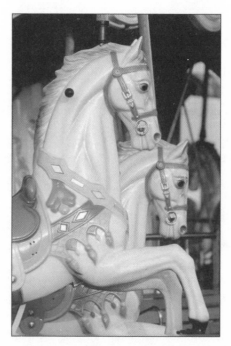

Merry-Go-Round horses, undated. SF

★   Oh, boy. In the 1950s or so, mentioning the Fair around the house was like one of us getting an award. Going to the Fair was the highlight of the summer. My husband and I would gather up our little ones and make a day of the Fair. I think I was as excited as they were. Of course their interest was the Midway and all of the good food. My husband and I liked all of the exhibits and the delicious sausage, pepper and onion sandwiches. The Fair would not be the same without them. We still enjoy it. What a wonderful way to end the summer. ***Jalica B. Housley***

★   When I was a little girl back in the 1920s and early 30s, going to the State Fair was a real occasion. Money was very tight, but five dollars was squeaked out of my Dad's pay to go to the Fair. Our five dollars paid the admission fee and the Grandstand seats. We went early in the morning and after viewing most of the buildings, we went back to the car at noon and ate the lunch my mother had packed. All of the parking then was on the grounds. After lunch we made our way to the Grandstand to watch the harness racing. That was my mother's favorite part of the whole day. As I walked by the ice cream stands, oh, how I wanted an "ice cream on a stick", but knew better than to ask as the money had been carefully planned. I don't walk by an ice cream stand to this day that I don't think about that. *Elizabeth Bowers*

★ When we were kids growing up in Solvay, New York, the biggest event to happen – next to the August 15th field days (Feast of the Assumption) – was the Great New York State Fair. The Fair always intrigued me, with the Midway workers, the oddities, the way they traveled and lived. And I admired how hard they worked. It also scared me a little.

In 1993, when General Motors shut down, we followed the job to Franklin, Tennessee. As sad as we all were, I was thinking in the back of my mind, "Okay, at least I can go back every year to the Fair and see everyone." It got better. I always wanted to have a concession at the Fair, to be involved in the excitement and be a part of the scene "behind the scene." So, when a concession opened up, we applied for the spots and I was thrilled to get in. Little did I know how fascinating it would be. It has become a big event each year. In just a few short years it has grown to mean a lot to my family and friends.

The best part is all the people who come to my booth. That is where I see my family, all of the people that I grew up with, who luckily still live there, all my life-long friends in Solvay and Camillus. My trips back each year are to my roots, and give me a sense of where I came from. All of the familiar people and sights are wonderful to see. A lot of us are grandparents and starting to retire. Where have the years gone? Even with so much changing in our lives the one thing that I can count on is when I go back to Solvay and the Fair it all looks and feels the same. *Sue Tacy Ostuni*

★ Boy, you've got us by the sneakers in bringing back memories of the New York State Fair. After doing some thinking, I remember being there once and in the Agricultural Exhibits when some man talked Donna into judging Potatoes. Well, it turned out that Donna won a prize, which was a 15 pound bag of potatoes. Guess who carried those potatoes around for most of the day? I didn't go to the car, because, I believe that we had parked clean the other side of the Thruway or at least it seemed that way. I think that was the last time that Donna ever judged potatoes, because I told her, "You ever win any more potatoes, it's your turn to carry them." **Bill and Donna Terry**

From the 1973 Fair official program book, a 1920 Ford, a New York State Police car, with the caption that the image "symbolizes the close, 56-year relationship between the New York State Police and the New York State Fair." NP

★ I am an attorney in the Syracuse area, but for two weeks each year, every year since I moved to Syracuse in 1988, I have been a bona fide Fair Rat. Up until about four years ago, I would go nearly every day to the Fair and have the parking stubs to prove it. Starting four years ago, I have made concerted efforts to find work at the fairgrounds; including spending one summer supervising garbage cleanup details. The past two years, I have managed to find a job at the Fair where I was not only able to be there all day, but I also got to sleep there and live there. Last year, my feet never touched soil outside the fairgrounds from the day before it started until midnight of the last night. Two years ago after the Fair ended, I sat down and wrote for nearly three hours recalling my experiences. Last year, I took my website "live" to the Fair and I was blogging events and experiences and feelings as they arose. Each Fair has its own unique attitude and ambiance. To me, it really is like Christmas – the noise, the lights, the hustle and bustle scurrying its way around you. As they say: "A bad day at the Fair beats a good day anywhere else". Nothing is as much fun as life at the Fair. **Mark David Blum**

★ One time after finishing tuning the piano for the Lawrence Welk band, I was standing back stage, lightly singing the words of his songs. This was maybe in 1997 and the Fair was using a Signer for the deaf that year. She saw that I was singing and asked me if I would stand behind her as the orchestra played and sing the words of the songs while she signed them for the deaf members of the audience. I agreed. At some point in that performance, she told the audience that this was some sort of history being made: a blind person singing words so that she could sign for the deaf. *Kenneth A. Williams*

★   My mother, Gladys Wall Olmstead, worked at the State Fair from the time she was eligible as a child until we moved to California when she was 34. When I was a little girl, we lived in Jordan. Every morning Mom would have a surprise from the Fair for my brother Willie and I from when she worked the night before: salt water taffy, something that one of the booths was giving away, cotton candy. It was a thrill for us. After I moved to California, I missed going to the Fair. I was thrilled to take my 10-month old son Timmy to the Fair in 1987, 31 years after I had last been there. It was modernized and all, but the atmosphere was the same and I loved it. *Marley Olmstead Bruegger*

★   Truth be told, I didn't appreciate the Fair until I was grown and had children of my own. I don't know why I resisted the Fair as a youngster, but I did. Later, when I worked at the Herald-Journal, I was assigned to cover the Fair and I think it made the Fair seem more like a chore than the fun it should have been. Eventually I came to appreciate the size and scope of an event I had previously taken for granted. Years later, while living out of state, I made a point of visiting my parents in Solvay at Fair time so I could introduce my children to the wonder of it all. *Jack Major*

★   I was eight when the Fair reopened after World War II. My siblings and I were allowed to attend by ourselves, with our bag lunches in hand. It was the best day of the year, next to Christmas and birthdays. Attendance would be poor this day, because of rain and a polio warning. It was a chance we would take.

I could eat free samples from the vendors all day, like a great treasure hunt to find my next hand-out. The ice-cold chocolate milk in the Dairy Building was a must. You could see the races from the second floor windows, people would climb on the roof of buildings and stands to watch the fast cars and the dirt from the track would cover everything. After the race, I'd check out every cage of funny ducks and birds in colors I was sure were not real. If we got tired, it was off to the horse show. I always sat as high in the Coliseum as possible. There we'd rest and eat our bag lunch. Tractors, pigs and cows, fly fishing contest in the pools on the main grounds, free shows, fudge and watching guys sell pots and pans and knives that would cut anything. We'd buy a dish to take to Mom.

The Midway was saved for last. Once there, what coin we had would soon be gone. This place I knew to be filled with fakers and trickery. Motorcycles driving around a huge barrel, that was two stories high, their wheels sending sparks, drove round and round defying gravity, and I'm sure damaging your ears. The Ring Masters selling their shows on a small stage outside their main tent. Dancers and fat ladies, snakes and charmers. The show was always just about to begin. The games, darts or rings, balls and milk bottles and the shooting gallery with a little red star for a target. Later in my life I actually shot it out. No prize. Just satisfaction. A straw cowboy hat I'd wear for twenty years, sandcastles and bees, politicians, street performances, trams pulled by tractors, Indian Village, little stools to vibrate sore feet and people, people everywhere – the best show.

Nine p.m., as late as it could get, we'd meet Dad at the main gate, take our treasures and memories home. There was never a bad day at the Fair. *John E. McLaughlin*

★   I have been going to the State Fair since I was a little girl, maybe since 1932. When I was in Mattydale Grammar School, the children were invited to perform at the Grandstand, making a huge American Flag. We each had a piece of cardboard – I think it was 24" by 24" – with part of the flag painted on it. They played music and we all held up the pieces at the same time to form the flag. It was very exciting. *Julia Tourtellotte*

★   My life-long infatuation with the Fair began in the early 1970s. Being a Solvay original, the Fair is in my backyard. Back then, I think, it ran only for one week, near my August 24 birthday. On my birthday, my dad would drive me down to the fairgrounds from our home on Cogswell Ave in Solvay. Eventually, as I got older, I would go with my family, or with my Granny, Vicki Savo, and her friends. With Granny, we always walked, leaving early in the morning and not going home until nightfall. On my thirty-seventh birthday, a black and white marquee sign at the Fair – on rotation all that day – displayed the following: "Happy Birthday" (on the front) and "Cathy Savo" on the back. That was at the 2000 New York State Fair. These days, I proudly take my vacation every August by walking to and from the NYS Fair, still from Cogswell Ave in Solvay. As I start to venture down the Cogswell Ave hill, this feeling comes over me. For 12 days, my ritual is the same. I get there about noon each day and do not leave until 11 p.m. I find my place on the patio at "Heroes and Legends Café" or, most importantly, on the "Dance Floor" and in-between acts with the Trooper friends I've made over the years at their exhibit. *Catherine Savo*

★   When we pulled into the main gate at the end of our bus ride to the Fair with our grandmother, it was overwhelming. We were there to start our adventure. We visited all of the Fair (this in the `60s), but Grandmother made sure we left enough time for the one thing we came for … a treat so simple and yet so anticipated. As I recall, it was found near the Midway, tucked away past the "I GOT IT" game.

We knew what we wanted. It was the wild and exotic flavors of suckers. Rows and rows of small apple baskets packed with suckers. They were one dollar for a dozen. There was coconut that actually had little coconut pieces in them. And pineapple that tasted so sweet you

From the 1997 Fair, a Black Angus being taken for a walk around the grounds. SF

could image being on a tropical island with each lick. And root beer, butterscotch, blueberry, raspberry and chocolate.

We each took our turn standing in front of the old apple baskets, laboring over our many choices. The little old man running the stand was patient, holding open our paper bag so we could fill it with exactly what we wanted. He never rushed us, but did offer occasional suggestions to move the process along. We each had a paper bag with twelve of the most carefully chosen treats.

Once we made our choices, they were ours – this was the one time of the year we didn't have to share with anyone. No need to hide them from my siblings. They had their own. As we walked back to the bus, Grandmother allowed us to have just one – and that posed a difficulty at times: which to have and which to save for later?

As the years passed, and I started taking my own children to the Fair, I always kept my eyes open for the little old man who stood next to his rows of lollipops calling out "Twelve for a dollar. Any flavor". *Kae Young*

★   The Fair was a wonderful end to our summer and I looked forward to it every year. I grew up in a family with five brothers and no sisters. We lived in Central Square on a farm and our trips to Syracuse were few and far between. However, I remember working and saving my money all summer for the trip to the State Fair. My parents would pack a lunch in our big silver cooler so that we could stay all day. We didn't have a lot of money in those days, so we'd walk back to the car and enjoy sandwiches and Kool-Aid in the shade while we rested up to go back and walk some more. One year I saved up enough money to buy a felt hat that had a big long feather and the vendor put my name on it with sparkles. We never visited the Midway for the rides until we were much older. All in all, we always had fun. We learned a lot by going to the State Fair. It was a wonderful place to visit when I was a child and I still love going there today. *Jill Ladd*

★   In Central New York, summer saves its most delicious treat for the last two weeks in August. It is then that the Empire Expo Center is transformed into a place where people of all ages can enjoy rides, eat all types of food, buy almost any product you can imagine, listen to music, watch animals, see talent shows, and do just about anything else their hearts' desire. I would be hard-pressed to choose my favorite State Fair

From the 1995 Fair, the sand sculpture. SF

memory. One thing about the Fair is guaranteed – you go home with a lot of goodies and with enough memories to last you through the winter months, and beyond. ***Heather Brady***

★ As a teenager, Mom and several of her friends at the time (including neighbor Betty Bartlett), would attend the Fair in style. They *had* to be cool, you know. This was the mid-'50s. The Fair was not yet paved, the Midway and other roads were dirt, and a girl never wore her best sneakers. However, she would not be caught without her new pair of Levi's.

The girls each had a US Navy issue *middy* blouse to wear, compliments of Betty Bartlett's elder brother Billy who had just been honorably discharged from the Navy. They each made scarves to match in various colors and paraded around the Fair in their look-alike outfits, feeling just as cool as could be. Note: the Bartlett family continues to be connected with the Fair with their impressive champion Bartlett Family Clydesdales, a "must see" for any Fair-goer these days. ***Catherine LaManna***

★ For over 60 years I have attended the New York State Fair and have seen many changes. Mostly the changes have appeared in the concession stands – which used to be tents. People I know tease me all the time when the Fair rolls around, asking me how many times I am going to go to the Fair that year. My answer is always, "as many times as I can." The only years I've missed going to the Fair were the four years I was in the Service. ***Tom Triscari***

★ It's amazing how some things never change. When I was a child, I would visit the State Fair every year with my mother and sister Cassie. Since we were so small, everything looked so big. We spent the day playing games, riding rides and of course eating. On one trip to the Fair, my mother's friend won large stuffed dogs for my sister and me. I still have both of them packed away in a closet.

Cassie and I used to like to play the goldfish game where you throw a ping-pong ball in the bowl and win a fish. While goldfish usually die quickly, one that we won at the Fair one year lasted almost two years. Before leaving the Fair, we would buy a treat to take home. Cassie always liked caramel apples but I preferred candy apples. Even after growing up and Cassie's relocation to Pennsylvania, whether together or separate, we went to the Fair at least once a year.

In 2004, I took my 2-year-old son to the Fair. He enjoys the animals, especially feeding carrots to the giraffes, but wouldn't you know? He liked the goldfish game. He also liked the "I GOT IT" game where you throw the balls in the grid and try to get them in a straight line before the rest of the players. Even as young as he is, the State Fair had him hooked on a favorite game. We ended up spending more money there than we planned, since he kept asking to play "just one more time". How could I say "no" with his grandmother there to spoil him? I look forward to taking him this year, as well as many to come. **Jenna LaManna**

★ My wife Valerie is so into the Fair she has been proclaimed by her friends and herself as the State Fair Princess. Valerie spends at least several days at the Fair, wearing out several different friends and myself trying to keep up with her there. She also makes a point each year to carefully study the gadgets from the Fair. Then she buys it/them, and then she spends the year telling everyone about it. We are so Fair orientated that we had a pot-luck "State Fair" party a few weeks ago celebrating the fact that the Fair is only six months away. Yes, Valerie organized it. We had Fair foods, including sausage/pepper and onion sandwiches, cheese curds, summer sausage (beef stick), apple dumpling *a la mode*, pizza *frete*, French fries, salt potatoes, hot dogs and coneys, beer and wine slushies. Valerie carried on so much about the Fair that our neighbor Matt Schnelee created a Butter Sculpture from four pounds of butter. We *like* the Fair. Valerie *loves* the Fair. **Alex Sokolowski**

★ The first time our family attended the New York State Fair was in the summer of 1989. Our youngest daughter Danielle's dance team had won a talent competition at the Wayne County Fair and they had been asked to perform in competition at the State Fair. Of course, the whole family made the trip, including teenager Deana (Danielle's sister) and her new boyfriend, father Gene and me. It was an hour-long drive to get there, and immediately on arrival, the teenagers headed for the Midway and rides. Gene and I strolled the grounds. Danielle and her friends had their own good time while waiting for their time to compete. We all enjoyed the lip smacking, finger-licking junk food that fairs have to offer. In the late afternoon, we reconnected to watch as Danielle and her teammates performed flawlessly. By then it had gotten colder and a drizzle prevailed. The competition ended for them but we had a glorious day at the Fair. **Susan Manno**

★ Long ago my two daughters and I explored the State Fair together. Martha was seven years old and Ginger was five. Our first stop, as always, was the Indian Village for they so much enjoyed the Indian dancers and always bought an article of beautiful beading. Following the Village we wandered around the grounds, buying ice cream and seeing various exhibits. All the animals received a good bit of their interest, especially the beavers, as I recall. But Ginger somehow strayed from Martha and me. All of a sudden she was nowhere to be seen. Panic. We tried to trace our steps, but *no Ginger*. We then went to the State Trooper's headquarters. There she was,

From the 1997 Fair, a Native American dancer in traditional dress at Indian Village. SF

as happy as a clam, eating pears – always her favorite fruit. What a relief. She wasn't the least bit scared, just took the separation all in stride. We stayed and continued to enjoy the Fair. **Marion Williams**

★   The Fair is the best place in the world. There are tons and tons of rides and food. Everywhere you look there are people smiling and laughing because they're having an awesome time. It's loads of fun. The food is great. You probably couldn't find one place with bad food. My favorite is pizza. The other best part of the Fair is the rides. **Ronn Bidwell**

★   We are real, self-proclaimed Fair "groupies". As an example, in 2004, on the Monday after we attended the Fair (on opening weekend), my husband Ted was in a car accident that landed him in the hospital. I had just flown out of Syracuse to New York City, and flew back immediately, of course. Ted's injuries were moderate but temporarily disabling. To boost his spirits, I promised him that I would get him back to the Fair by the upcoming weekend. And we did, with Ted experiencing the Fair from the wheelchair perspective. **Laura Rozelsky**

★   It might just be me, but it seems that the Fair has a distinct smell – a wonderful conglomeration of fried food, lake air, animals, and the hot August sun. In a flash that scent takes me to 24-or-so Fairs-gone-by, and to sights of baby chicks, rabbit shows, and crowing roosters. I am riding the Ferris Wheel and tasting a warm apple dumpling. I develop an urge to have a 25¢ milk (the best milk in the world) from the Rainbow Milk Bar and see a butter sculpture (how do they do that?). I feel the allure of the Midway (arguably the heart of the Fair – where else can you win live fish and stuffed animals and also buy clothing and house wares?) and can close my eyes and see the final, spectacular fireworks light-show of the Fair. **Heather Brady**

★   When the subject of the Fair comes up at work, my colleagues all say, "If you want to know where things are at the Fair, just ask Carol. She goes every day." It's a fact.

I don't know how anyone can see everything without going every day … so I do. I get a multiple day pass, use any extra tickets people offer and make sure I have my hand stamped in case I want to go back at night. To keep costs down, I have someone drop me off near an entrance instead of parking. Give-aways of pens and paper can fill your bags, along with lots of informative reading materials – something for everyone. Resting frequently and watching others enjoy the Fair is fun, too. The nights with the fireworks are wonderful.

I plan each day at the Fair so that I can enjoy the demonstrations, displays and concerts without being rushed. For example… you can usually see the high dive, circus and concert in easily in one afternoon, because they are all located in one area. My visits to the buildings are spread out over 2-3 days; another day for the animals and of course a day just for the Midway. The last day brings me to the Fair as soon as the gates open. I have breakfast and walk around for the last time that year. Now everything looks familiar to me, so the leisurely walk is a review to last me until next year. The State Fair – I love it.

So how about it? Anyone have an extra ticket? **Carol L. Cook**

The present Main Gate at the Fair. JPL

The State Fair Stories Story

Christmas sales of *Solvay Stories* (both I and II) had just begun to settle-down. I was happily at work on my novel. But something possessed me, compelled me, to call the New York State Fair. A story from Solvay classmate Sue Tacy Ostuni contributed for *Solvay Stories II* was on my mind. Sue returns annually to work at the State Fair, even though she moved out of state. My niece Cassie loved the Fair and would come home from Pennsylvania to spend a week of daily visits there. My sister Carol goes to the Fair *every* day. Bring up the Fair and people young and old tell of their State Fair traditions. It made sense to collect their memories.

In early January of this year I called the Fair Director's office. Joan Kerr (I now call her "Joan at the Fair") answered and I began to introduce myself. "My name is Judith LaManna Rivette and…" .

"Oh, yes. I know who you are," she interrupted. "You wrote the Solvay books."

"Oh," (aren't I articulate?)

"We loved them," she added, "I'm from Solvay."

"Ah," (this I thought to myself) and then clarified, "What's your Solvay name?"

She understood. "Balduzzi. Class of `68."

"The reason for this call – this is just tentative, mind you," I explained, "is that I'm wondering if there might be an interest in having a book like *Solvay Stories* about the State Fair. What do you think?" After that, Joan talked to Fair Director Peter Cappuccilli, who, by the end of January had two meetings with me, including some of his staff. The plan from the start was that *State Fair Stories* would be a collection of memories from as early as possible to the present. I made a commitment to produce this book for sale at this year's Fair.

For me, *State Fair Stories* is a natural progression from the *Solvay Stories* books. There are State Fair chapters in the first two *Solvay Stories* books, and this book holds some stories that were submitted for *Solvay Stories II*. Solvay and the fairgrounds are connected geographically. Most Solvay children still walk to the Fair and generations of Solvay families have been employed at the fairgrounds.

Much of the staff at the Fair has shared Peter's enthusiasm for this project. All was open to me to see, touch, ask about. Their community is like a family, with a very long history and memory of its own that some were kind enough to share for this book.

The collections of Peter Cappuccilli and Nick Pirro, Jr., provided a trove of old photos and memorabilia to share. The help of Joan Kerr was endless, insight and support came from Millie Bankert, Jim Goss, Linda Ryan; story source suggestions and/or technical support came from Mary Ellen Daino, Mary Ellen Chesbro and Emmy Moss. Nick walked the Fair with my niece Jenna LaManna while she took photos; he maneuvered me through the State Fair web site and he opened doors for me – literally – around the grounds.

It is a tribute to the efforts of Peter Cappuccilli in particular that people with special needs and children who might not have had contact with the Fair have been embraced by this project. For me, it has been a delight to have "met" some people associated with those special needs. It will be a true pleasure to re-meet them, face-to-face, at a book signing or sale. I hope to also meet a surprise set of contributors who wrote because of the efforts of Solvay Schools Teacher Deborah Samuel, who figured (correctly) that the possibility of being in a book was a strong motivator when she assigned her class to write a Fair story: results were selected stories from Ronn Bidwell, James Cerio, Brenin Matticio, Sean Mulholland, Jared Ott, Seth Randall, Kevin Revette II, Fallon Rogers, Amy Ruszczak and Sandra Simmons.

The pictures in this book are a collection of old and new. Once again, Solvay Library came through with some interesting old photos, including a choice of those of the Process lime bed break. I elected to not include group photos because of page size and identification limitations.

As I noted in the Brief History chapter, credit for early collection of State Fair and fairgrounds history goes to others. My efforts only summarize that history in a broad sweep. I am not a true historian, but I hope I have helped to fill-in history, anecdotally, in my own way.

The local media has been of tremendous help in publicizing my various "*Story*" efforts. To advertise collecting the stories, Peter and I appeared together on *Bridge Street* (Channel 9) and on *Our CNY* (Channel 24). I sat with Laura Hand (Channel 5) and was on the Rick and Amy Show (Y94 FM). My friends Jim O'Hara and Dick Case find ways to squeeze news about my efforts into their columns. The Syracuse New Times amazes me annually with the talented writing of an intern – this year it was Luke Mullins, whose piece announcing the collecting of stories produced a significant response.

Encouragement and help has never been at ebb: a call to Barry Shulman for a missing name; office and organizing help from Jenna, Lisa Lorch and Mary Ellen Daino; story source suggestions from former WRVO reporter Skye Rhode and reporter Dick Case and encore proof reading by Lisa Lorch and Barbara Rivette.

All of this has caused *State Fair Stories* to appear on time.

My books continue to be sold at Solvay Library and book stores. As information changes, it appears on my Web Site (www.solvaystories.com), which is under the constant care and attention of Joey Simon, my "webmeister."

The stories for this book appeared in response to a huge flier mailing and a generosity of local media attention. The results are that this book has over 100 contributors and I may already have a start on *State Fair Stories II*. No kidding.

With that, I end this story. But not without eliciting your promise to send me more stories, enough more for me to collect and share with all. I can always use pictures of the places and events of the Fair and fairgrounds, old and new, and hope to collect more of those, too.

Over these past few months, I have felt like a new member of the State Fair family and of the families of many contributors. There is never enough time to talk with people about their memories, but had I not restricted my interview time I'd never have gotten around to writing. It continues to be a source of deep satisfaction to learn that my story collections help make care-giving for older relatives a little more pleasant, the memories offering a distraction from daily routines, aches and medications, providing different topics for conversation.

With our sudden loss of my niece Cassie this past fall, it has been a hard year on our family. It has been a help to us to have the distraction of creating this book. *State Fair Stories* has been a warming and joyful endeavor, and I thank all for their help. **Judith LaManna Rivette**

Names Index

Note: The names of contributor "story-tellers" are in bold print. Names mentioned in full are in non-bold. Names of restaurants, stands, buildings or general reference to a family by only first or last name are not listed. Where several members of a family appear in one story, they are listed together. With apology for names missed in this Index.

Adams, Agnes – 98
Amidon, Reta – 48
Atkinson, Kristen and Michele – 23
Avery, Jean – 97
Baldwin, Steven – 72
Bankert, Millie – 25, 30, 34, 73, 94, 99, 119
Baratta, Jessie – 19
Barnello, Richard (Barney) – 54
Bartlett, Betty – 113
Bechard, K.C. Cerio – 6, 35
Bidwell, Ronn – 116, 119
Blasi, Mary – 131
Blum, Mark David – 50, 60, 98, 104, 108
Bowers, Elizabeth – 20, 107
Brady, Heather – 18, 27, 49, 59, 98, 113, 116
Brandt, Susan Mascette – 54, 72, 77, 82, 88, 104
Braunstein, Ben – 57
Brouillette, Karen and Rudy – 24
Brown, Weiner – 82
Bruegger, Marley Olmstead – 44, 109
Bryant, Anita –39

Burton, Shamone – 8, 22, 97, 105
Buzze, Annabelle – 55
Caffrey, Charmaine – 11, 27, 41, 60
Caffrey, Tony – 60
Campbell, Jane – 58
Campbell, Marty – 87
Capone, Al - 71
Cappuccilli, Peter – vii, x, xi, 72, 103, 118, 119
Carducci, Rudy – 54
Case, Dick – 7, 33, 36, 55, 57, 64, 69, 74, 102, 120
Caselle, Corky (Patrick) – 10
Cash, Johnny - 91
Castellani, Joe – 43, 86
Cavallero, Helen and Fort – 53
Cerio, James – 56, 119
Cerio, Nickie and Don – 6
Charron, Claude – 82
Chesboro, Mary Ellen – 35, 119
Chiaferri, Rocco – 75
Clifford, David – 41
Clinton, Chelsea – 71
Clinton, Senator Hillary – 15, 16, 71, 72

From the 1951 Fair, the front and back of the Pupil Ticket. PC

Clinton, President William – 15, 16, 72

Colella, Lenny – 90

Colella, Stan – 90

Cook, Carol L. – 48, 117, 118

Cook, Russell – 50, 58

Cooper, Michelle – 58

Cooper, Rev. Thomas – 68

Creal, Harold – 81, 83

Cuomo, Andrew – 72

Cuomo, Mario – 72

Daino, Mary Ellen – 27, 28, 47, 66, 94, 103, 119, 120

Daino, Melissa – 47

Davis, Beverly – 8, 11, 27, 51

Delfavero, Bill – 54

DeLucia, Judith Conway – 50, 53, 58, 86

Demperio, Thomas R. –viii, 11, 57, 79, 86, 96

Despard, Andy – 82

Dewey, Governor Thomas – 71

Doherty, Mary Davis – 53

Doran, Robert – 14, 88

Draper, Gail – 18, 63

Duncan, Arthur – 90

Earhart, Amelia – 73

Eckler, Cali, Kelsey and Tori – 23

Eckler, Phyllis A. – 23

Edison, Al – 63

Ehland, Kaitlin – 23

Ennis, Donald – 70, 79

Ennis, Noah – 70, 79

Falcone, William – 70, 73

Farley, Postmaster Gen. James – 73

Feeney, John – 42

Ford, Tennessee Ernie – 39

Forger, Dick – 32, 78

Foyt, A.J. – 81

Frakes, Nancy – 76

Franchini, Joe – 54

Fredericks, Bill – 7, 9, 12, 40, 69, 93, 101

PC

Fulmer, Lillian and Fred – 62

Gable, Clark – 44

Gallagher, Wayne – 27

Gallante, Bill – 77

Gallante, Dey (Daniel) – 54

Gettino, Danny – 77

Gigliotti, Tony – 16

Glenister, Gabrielle – 29

Goeghan, Whitie – 82

Gordon, Brooke and Jeff – 72

Goss, Jim – 66, 70, 119

Greco, Tommy – 54

Greene, Nina, Orville and Kehala – 70

Hampton, Lyonel – 41

Hand, Laura – 120

Hanlon, Jeremy – 30, 32

Harriman, Governor Averell – 73
Hoffman, Dustin - 72
Housley, Jalica – 106
Howe, John B. – 35
Hughes, Governor – 73
Iannuzzi, Barbara Phillips – 66
Isgar, Billy – 67
Jakowski, Jake – 13
Jarrett, Dale – 69
Jones, Paul – 24
Kafka, Sergeant – 41
Kanasola, Bob – 12
Kay, Sammy – 39
Keating, Senator Kenneth – 88
Kennedy, Bobby – 71
Kerr, Joan Balduzzi – vii, 118, 119
Killecut, Bette Hughes – 25
Klamm, Edward - 88
Klein, Kristen – 11, 39
Klodzen, Joe – 12, 91
Ladd, Beverly and Rip – 7
Ladd, Jill – 7, 28, 48, 112
La Manna Rivette, Judith (see
    Rivette, Judith La Manna)
La Manna, Catherine – 30, 51, 113
La Manna, Fran – 131
La Manna, Frank – 12
La Manna, Jenna – vii, 70, 114, 119
La Manna, John – 86
La Manna, Rose and Frank – 131
La Penna, Frank – 54
Lauricella, Richard – 20
Lawler, Kathy – 102
Lee, Gypsy Rose – 39
Lehman, Governor Herbert – 18
Litz, Deacon – 43
Long, Louie – 89
Lorch, Lisa – 120
Lotito, Brenda – 24, 52
Lowe, Cliff – 87
Lucas, AJ and Patrick – 44, 81
Lucas, Barbara – 31, 76, 78, 81

SF

Luchsinger, John – 20
Luczyski, Kay – 54
Magner, Tracey Leigh – 66
Major, Jack – 8, 34, 44, 52, 83, 92,
    109
Manno, Susan – 115
Mara, Roger – 94
Martin, Mark – 69
Mascette, Alice M. – 91, 103
Mascette, Paul – 34
Mascetti, Helen – 77
Mascetti, Zinzi – 66, 77, 90, 91
Matthews, Buttes – 10
Matticio, Brenin – 60, 119
Maxwell, Bette and Robert – 104
May, Bob – 83

Maziuk, Joanne – 52
McEntire, Reba – 72, 73
McGinn, Bess – 85
McKinley, President – 73
McLaughlin, David – 84
McLaughlin, John E. – 87, 110
Merritt, Judy Wilson – 20
Mezzo, Fannie and Sam – 54
Miguel, Pepe – 77
Mikan, George – 83
Miller, Greg – 65
Miller, Stacey – 13
Mills, Harriet May – 35
Mills, Henry – 35
Moberg, Karl – 8
Monti, Rose and Charlie – 14
Morgan, Dick – 41, 42
Moss, Emmy – 119
Mulholland, Sean – 82, 119
Mullins, Luke – 120
Murray, Ann – 40

Murphy, Mark – 21
Neary, Don – 59
Neary, John – 23, 32, 46, 59
Neary, Tom – 23
Nelson, Gladys – 22
Nesci, Karen – 63
Nichols, William – 26, 27, 90
Nicit, Norine – 60
Nicolini, Rich – 34
O'Hara, Jim – 120
O'Hara, Joe – 103
O'Leary, Jimmy – 14
O'Neil, Frances Wall – 11, 89
Okoniewski, Mike – vii
Olgeaty, May – 53, 57
Olgeaty, Thelma – 53
Olmstead, Gladys Wall – 109
Ostuni, Susan Tacy – 15, 72, 92,
    100, 105, 107, 118
Ott, Jared – 60, 119
Palerino, Vince – 54, 90

JLR

Pannetti, Pat – 54
Parsons, Johnnie – 81
Pataki, Governor George – x, 72, 79, 102
Patton, Thomas G. – 18
Patuna, Fred – 62
Petrella, Dan – 10
Phillips, Mona – 55, 66
Phillips, Ron – 54
Pierce, John – 35
Pirro, County Executive Nick – 9
Pirro, Nick Jr. – vii, 9, 102, 119
Pyle, Gomer – 28
Randall, Seth – 32, 119
Rebhan, John – 36
Reddy, Helen – 96, 97
Reep, Josh – 102
Revette II, Kevin – 58, 119
Rhode, Skye – 120
Rinaldi, Susan and Jerry – 68
Rivers, Bernard – 87, 97
Rivers, Jean – 96
Rivette, Barbara S. – 17, 35, 45, 93, 120
Rivette, Frances R. – vii, 13, 44, 131
Rivette, Judith La Manna – x, 12, 37, 44, 78, 80, 87, 118, 120
Rockefeller, Governor Nelson – 25, 73, 88, 93

Rogers, Fallon – 59, 119
Romano, Karen Nicolini – 14, 34
Roosevelt, President Theodore – 73
Root, Mary Kay – 64
Rossi, Eliseo – 63
Rozelsky, Laura and Ted – 28, 53, 79, 98, 116
Ruszczak, Amy – 30, 119
Ruth, Brian – 89
Ryan, Linda – 62, 119
Salmon, Christa – 27
Salvetti, Don (Saggy) – 54
Samuel, Deborah – 119
Savo, Catherine – 28, 111
Savo, Vicki – 110
Schnelee, Matt – 114
Schramm, Henry W. – 4, 63
Schoeneck, Lieut. Governor Edward – 8
Seabrook, Wendy and Paul – 68, 102
Segar, Elizabeth Szczech – 51
Shapiro, Rob – 94
Shea, Charles F. – 68
Shea, James and John – 68
Sherman, Vice President James – 73
Shulman, Barry – 120
Simiele, John – 54
Simon, Joey – 120

Simmons, Sandra – 40, 119
Sinatra, Frank Jr. – 100
Skvorak, Jim and Cathy – 39
Smith, Arriana – 70
Smolinski, Tom – 34, 91
Snyder, Jenny and Wilbur – 62
Sobon, Mary Lou – 105

Sokolowski, Valerie and Alex – 114
Spears, Brittany – 42
Sprague, Corky – 65
Stankwicz, Walter – 43
Strates, James – 57, 65, 72
Strickland, Helen – 89
Szczech, John – 50

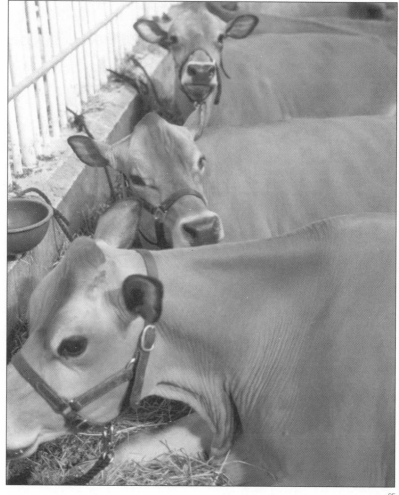

SF

Taft, Present William Howard – 73
Tarolli, Harmon - 77
Teeter, Lucky – 44, 45
Terry, Donna and Bill – 108
Tickner, Marion – 48, 63
Tim, Tiny – 39
Tindall, Arthur – 7, 12, 58
Tourtellotte, Julia – 40, 110
Triscari, Tom – 71, 113
Tucci, Lucie, Mary and Rudy – 54
Tuzzolino, Angie and Patti – 67
Tuzzolino, Kathy – 67
Vail, Jerry – 39
Vandervort, Helen Bull – 71, 88,
Victor, Jim – 31, 32
Walker, Jimmy – 87
Wall, Robert E. – 95, 104
Walton, Miriam Witter – 73
Warren, Mr. – 63

Wells, Madge – 39, 53, 57, 64, 65,
   73, 93
Wheeler, Harold C. – 67, 69, 81,
   94
Wheeler, Harold D. and Harry – 69
White, Cassie La Manna – 114,
   118, 120
Widger, Bruce – 18
Williams, Kenneth A. – 39, 50, 90,
   109
Williams, Marion – 116
Willoughby, Frank – 86
Willoughby, Mayola – 14, 52, 99
Wilson, Jennie – 20
Witter, Daniel Parrish – 73
Wrightsman, Maureen – 86
Yoder, John – 54
Young, Kae – 112
Young, Tom – 94

Afterword

The New York State Fair has been a valuable part of our history, heritage, family and community. These pages have offered you only a tiny portion of the voices and memories of that history, that community, that experience.

Thank you for your support of Youth Day and Special Needs Services at the Fair through your purchase of this volume.

Collecting these memories and preparing this book has given me a deeper appreciation of the history and humanity that is behind the operations of the New York State Fair. To those who have entrusted their memories to my handling, I hope I have given that trust the care it deserves.

Perhaps reading these stories has helped you to remember a special memory or two or has given you some unexpected connection in time. If you have a memory you wish to share and/or some photos, please send them to me at the address below. With enough additional stories, photos and memories, there will be a second volume. Then will have the pleasure of seeing you again next year at the New York State Fair.

Judith La Manna Rivette

ENTERPRISES

200 Old Liverpool Road
Liverpool, NY 13088
www.solvaystories.com

About the Author

Like hundreds of Solvay children before me, I walked to the Fair practically daily, an end of summer tradition. We went over the old, iron-span Bridge Street bridge, that shook when cars sped by. There were holes in the sidewalk near the top of the bridge that you could look down through and see the trains below. No matter. We – my brother and I or my girlfriends and I or my boyfriend and I – were on our way to the Fair.

My father Frank LaManna sometimes worked as an auxiliary policeman and directed traffic in Solvay during Fair-week, often at the corner of Milton Ave and Bridge St. My mother Rose LaManna volunteered, along with my Aunt Fran LaManna and, later, my Aunt Mary Blasi, to work at the Solvay Tigers' stand at the Fair, with long hours of standing, cooking, serving and a lot of laughing.

Between my summers at the Fair, my education was local – Onondaga Community College, LeMoyne College and Syracuse University. In 1983 I became an attorney and I have been a Labor Arbitrator since 1978. My other work is writing, which is hardly work at all, including *Solvay Stories* and *Solvay Stories II,* both of which were named Local Best Sellers. When I am not working or writing, I draw cartoons, tap dance, bake bread and pies and go to some pretty interesting car shows and events.

In 1983 I married my best friend, Ric (Francis) Rivette. From our home in Liverpool, we are about directly across Onondaga Lake from the New York State Fair. We can see the fireworks displays of the Fair from our front porch. How good is that?

Other
Publications

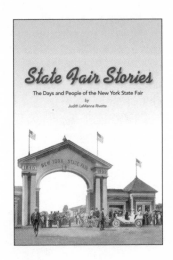

To order:

Solvay Stories: *A 100-Year Diary of Solvay, New York, its Days and its People (2003)*

Solvay Stories II: *More from the Diary of Solvay, New York (2004)*

State Fair Stories: *the Days and People of the New York State Fair (2005)*

Mail a check or money order ($24 per book – this includes tax, postage and handling) payable to:

Oh, How Upstate
200 Old Liverpool Road
Liverpool, NY 13088

along with a note summarizing
your order and including your mailing address.